INTERROGATING
CHINESE ROCK

Lei (Nada) Peng

INTERROGATING CHINESE ROCK

A Cross-Cultural Journey Integrating Research and Identity

Cultural Anthropology
Collection Editors

Nila Ginger Hofman & Janise Hurtig

First published in 2025 by Lived Places Publishing

All rights reserved. No part of this publication may be reproduced, stored in a retrieval system, or transmitted in any form or by any means, electronic, mechanical, photocopying, recording, or otherwise, without prior permission in writing from the publisher.

No part of this book may be used or reproduced in any manner for the purpose of training artificial intelligence technologies or systems. In accordance with Article 4(3) of the Digital Single Market Directive 2019/790, Lived Places Publishing expressly reserves this work from the text and data mining exception.

The author and editors have made every effort to ensure the accuracy of the information contained in this publication, but assume no responsibility for any errors, inaccuracies, inconsistencies, or omissions. Likewise, every effort has been made to contact copyright holders. If any copyright material has been reproduced unwittingly and without permission, the publisher will gladly receive information enabling them to rectify any error or omission in subsequent editions.

Copyright © 2025 Lived Places Publishing

British Library Cataloguing in Publication Data
A CIP record for this book is available from the British Library.

ISBN: 9781916704497 (pbk)
ISBN: 9781916704510 (ePDF)
ISBN: 9781916704503 (ePUB)

The right of Lei (Nada) Peng to be identified as the Author of this work has been asserted by them in accordance with the Copyright, Design and Patents Act 1988.

Cover design by Fiachra McCarthy
Book design by Rachel Trolove of Twin Trail Design
Typeset by Newgen Publishing, UK

Lived Places Publishing
P.O. Box 1845
47 Echo Avenue
Miller Place, NY 11764

www.livedplacespublishing.com

The root of suffering is our false belief in a solid, separate, substantial self.

— Buddhist teaching on *anattā* (illusion of self)

Abstract

Interrogating Chinese Rock chronicles author Lei (Nada) Peng's autoethnographic journey as a Chinese rock listener and researcher between mainland China, France, and the United Kingdom. Bridging scholarly analysis and lived experience, this work traces how rock – a Western genre – is reimagined within China's socio-political landscape. It explores the dynamic interplay between Chinese rock music, cultural hybridity, global power structures, and personal identity, positioning music as a site of resistance, mystification, and self-discovery. Through an interdisciplinary lens, it challenges narratives of authenticity, ideological restriction, neoliberal globalisation, and interrogates the tensions between artistic expression, national identity, power, and belonging. This work also explores the ways in which the author navigates cross-cultural currents to forge identities that defy rigid categorisation.

Key words

autoethnography; centre and periphery; Chinese rock music; Chinese social transformation; cross-cultural identity integration; culture imperialism; fluid belonging; global power structures; marginal voices; music and society

Contents

Preface	ix
Acknowledgements	xv
Learning objectives	xxi
Introduction	xxii
Prelude: My encounter with rock 'n' roll in the People's Republic of China – A call for self-awareness	1
PART I Understanding Chinese rock, or *Yaogun*: A socio-political history and metaphor for 'identity searching'	9
Chapter 1 The rise of Chinese rock: A vessel for collective aspirations and echoes of individual liberation	15
Chapter 2 Constructing myth: Revolutionary narrative of rock	27
Chapter 3 Unveiling the myth of *Yaogun*: A reassessment of rock's 'periphery'	41
Chapter 4 'China Fire' under the 'Modern Sky': Transforming Chinese society before the dawn of a new century	69
Chapter 5 'New Sound of Beijing' and '*Dakou* generation': 'New clothes, new life!'	95

Interlude: From *Dakou* to the 'new era' – Navigating the spectacle of 'Chinese independent music' and the unfinished journey   **121**

PART II   Cross-cultural identity in motion: Navigating the journey from 'me' to 'us'   **127**

Chapter 6	Leaving home: From Kunming to Beijing – The awareness of centre and periphery	**129**
Chapter 7	Departing China for France: The second move and the disillusionment of an 'enlightened Europe'	**147**
Chapter 8	Departing France for England: The third move and the disillusionment with the 'liberal world'	**169**

The unfinished finale: From 'me' to 'us' – Metamorphosis of cross-cultural identity integration   **197**

Suggested projects, assignments, and discussion questions   **217**

Notes   **223**

References   **227**

Recommended further readings   **236**

Index   **239**

Preface

This book is an unfinished artifact – a living fragment of my cross-cultural journey, shaped by nearly two decades of intertwining academic inquiry into Chinese rock music and the relentless excavation of my own identity. It is not a conclusion but a testament to motion: a pilgrimage that has been as much about intellectual rigor as it has been about spiritual awakening.

This journey has been neither linear nor solitary. It is marked by the friction of existing as a persistent 'other' standing 'in-between': a Chinese woman challenging gendered expectations in the male subcultures of rock; an unmarried and childfree scholar defying societal scripts of femininity across borders; a migrant navigating the invisible hierarchies of Europe. Each confrontation with marginalisation became a mirror, reflecting to me the fractures of a world obsessed with labels – nation, race, class, gender – and the systems that weaponise them. Yet in those fractures, I also glimpsed light: the possibility of a self and a society, unshackled from the illusion of separation.

From the outset, my exploration of Chinese rock – a genre born of rebellion, dissonance, and a collective quest for personal freedom and authenticity, and imbued with many revolutionary and Enlightenment myths – mirrored my own quest to reconcile the fractures within myself. To study this music phenomenon was to confront questions of resistance, belonging, and voice in a society oscillating between collective conformity and individual yearning. Yet as I delved deeper, the chords of academia and spirituality began to harmonise. Through Buddhism and Taoism, I encountered teachings on impermanence, non-self, and non-attachment. These teachings reframed my understanding of identity, not as a fixed monument, but as a river – fluid, adaptive, and perpetually carving new paths through the bedrock of culture, politics, and memory.

This realisation emerged alongside my personal struggles, which were multi-layered. As a Chinese teenager, my love of rock music was an act of rebellion against a society deeply rooted in collectivist thinking and hierarchical order. As a woman, being a rock enthusiast in China – whether as a fan or a musician – was both 'cool' and alienating, forcing me to navigate a male-dominated subculture that often marginalised my presence and voice. Later, as an independent, unmarried, and childfree scholar, I confronted the gender violence of contemporary China's mixed feudal-neoliberal-patriarchal order, which relegates women who defy traditional roles to the symbolic periphery – labelled 'too tough', 'weird', or even gendered as 'the third sex'. Under neoliberalism's commodification of identity and the state's reinforcement of 'family values' in contemporary China and many other places, women like me face intensified exclusion; our refusal to sign the silent emotional contract that centres marriage or motherhood as core values for women renders us deviant. Yet, in hooks' terms, the periphery is also a site of radical possibility. My defiance – as a rock fan, as a scholar, as an independent thinker and spiritual seeker, as a woman unwilling to shrink – becomes a way of reclaiming agency from the margins.

Moving to Europe further deepened my awareness of the divisions between 'centre' and 'periphery'. As an Asian woman with no pre-established social capital, I encountered invisible barriers – glass doors – in everyday life, from finding housing to pursuing an academic path to securing employment. These experiences highlighted the intersection of race, gender, and class as key factors in marginalisation, whether in China's state-controlled market logic, France's 'egalitarian' ideals, or the neoliberal diversity of the United Kingdom.

In these pages, the personal and the political, the scholarly and the spiritual converge. This is not a story of arrival, but of becoming – a chronicle of how the study of music, critical inquiry, the practice of mindfulness and self-regulation, alongside the labour of cross-cultural survival can dissolve the boundaries between the many labels I have been assigned and to which I have adhered, revealing their inextricable dance.

Through nearly two decades of research, movements, lived experiences, and reflection, I have come to understand that the most marginalised people are often found at the intersection of these divides. The more I questioned the labels that were meant to define me – 'model student', 'rock girl', migrant, Asian, neo middle class, 'woman PhD' – the more I glimpsed the spaces between them. In Buddhist meditation, I sat with the ache of feeling 'invisible' in Europe, the sting of being 'too much' in China, slowly recognising them not as personal failures but as symptoms of a world obsessed with separation. My research into Chinese rock music also revealed this tension: musicians shouting against societal constraints, yet reproducing gendered, regional, and class hierarchies in their subculture. It mirrored my own struggle – to resist being pigeonholed by others while confronting the 'boxes' I'd internalised.

To move forward, my path required reimagining belonging not as a battle between 'me' and 'them', but as a mosaic of interdependencies. It meant seeing my 'rebellious' teenage self, my 'foreigner/immigrant' self, my 'single woman scholar' self, my 'spiritual seeker' self, not as conflicting identities, but as currents in the same river – shaped by culture, yes, but also shaping it. This is the heart of my autoethnographic reckoning: a refusal to let the world's fractures become my own.

This vision is not merely theoretical; it arises from my lived experience of integrating opposing narratives into my way of being. My cross-cultural journey – from China to France to the United Kingdom – has been about more than surviving as an 'Other' in both 'home' and 'foreign' lands. It has been about embodying and integrating this 'Otherness' within myself, in an ongoing process of transformation with no fixed destination. Two decades of cross-cultural journeys and academic and personal inquiry have led me to the conclusion that to cultivate a future of peace and harmony, we must bridge the gap between mind, heart, and action, aligning our conceptual understanding with practical life. Without this harmony, we remain isolated, unable to connect meaningfully as a collective.

I have come to see that this journey involves work in two intertwined frameworks: the conceptual and the practical. At the theoretical level, I draw from a variety of intellectual and philosophical traditions: critical theory, as articulated by Michel Foucault, which challenges power structures and questions subjectivity; postcolonial perspectives, particularly those of Frantz Fanon, Homi Bhabha, James Baldwin, Edward Said, and Arundhati Roy, which critique imperialism in all its forms, interrogate the psychological legacies of colonialism, and unravel the complexities of hybrid identities and cultural 'third spaces' (Bhabha, 1994); Buddhist and Taoist notions of *non-self*, which emphasise interdependence and the futility of ego-driven self-attachments; feminist and queer studies, informed by thinkers like bell hooks, Dai Jinhua, and Chizuko Ueno, which challenge patriarchal, neoliberal, and orthodox norms while imagining new ways of living, caring, and reclaiming agency as individual and as community. These theoretical tools provided me with the conceptual grounding necessary to understand identity beyond rigid boxes and binaries.

Yet theory alone is insufficient.

On a practical level, this journey requires introspection and connection. It means asking myself: 'How am I feeling? How am I relating to others? Am I listening without judgement? How can I help without imposing my views and values?' Practices like meditation, journaling, and spending time in solitude provide a foundation, but so does fostering connection with others – seeking common ground, showing vulnerability, offering empathy, and sharing struggles. This unity of theory and practice – a grounding praxis – has been central to my process of intercultural identity integration.

From Kunming, China to Lyon, France to Liverpool, England, from a young girl enchanted by rock music to an academic navigating cultural, social, and political narratives, I have learnt that there is no fixed 'true self' to discover. Instead, there are countless 'selves' in constant flux, shaped by encounters, reflections, and struggles. This insight aligns with Buddhist teachings on non-self (*anattā*) and emptiness (*śūnyatā*), which assert that the self is fluid, without a fixed essence, constantly changing in response to its conditions.

In recognising this *non-self*, I have found a deeper sense of belonging – not as an attached component of a family, work unit, ethnical group, or nation, but as part of a shared human journey. Moving from 'me' to 'us' is not about losing oneself; it is about embracing a collective ground, finding strength in interdependence, and acknowledging our interconnected struggles. In an increasingly divided world, where technology and dualistic ideology threaten our very existence and the environment in which we live, this understanding feels more urgent than ever.

Perhaps it is in *emptiness* – free of rigid identities and conventional narratives – that we can begin to imagine a new Self, as elaborated in Carl Jung's (1968) framework. Perhaps it is from a 'ground zero' of invisibility, where we detach from the ego, that we can imagine a world beyond existing binaries.

Ultimately, this book is driven by a deep aspiration, inspired by the Buddhist tradition of setting intentions:

> May we never seek to be seen through the eyes of those who refuse to see us.
> May we never cling to the illusion of a solid, separate, and substantial self, but find ourselves in the fluidity of interdependence – interwoven with others, nature, and the cosmos, like a raindrop dissolving into the infinite ocean of wholeness.

Acknowledgements

> How do you keep a drop of water from drying up? Just put it in the ocean.
>
> – Engraved on a stone in the film *Samsara* (Pan Nalin, 2001)

This quote above first anchored my doctoral acknowledgements a decade ago, a testament to five years of solitary, self-funded struggle. Today it resurfaces as I complete this book – a project born out of that thesis, but deepened by another decade of wandering across a different landscape. Today, at a time when the world is fracturing into deeper conflict and division, the metaphor holds even more strongly: like a single drop sustained by the ocean, this work exists only through the boundless support of countless elements and souls that have shaped my journey.

I extend my deep gratitude to Professor Gregory Lee, whose open-minded guidance and intellectual rigour were the nurturers of my critical voice in France. His unwavering faith in his vision of transcultural studies, coupled with his passion for bridging academia and lived experience, provided the intellectual foundation for this book.

I cannot forget the scholars who stimulated my academic curiosity during my years at Peking University. Among them, I am thinking in particular of Professor Dai Jinhua 戴锦华, who not only inspired and motivated me to explore issues related to cultural studies but also encouraged me to relate these explorations to my own life experiences and reflections. I remain deeply grateful for the opportunity to attend many of her lectures and seminars as an immature and naive student at Peking University.

I was captivated by her profound knowledge, charismatic eloquence, and her egalitarian grace – how she welcomed every question with warmth, dissolving hierarchies between teacher and student. I will never forget her response to my fumbling question nearly 20 years ago – 'What is ideology?'; she answered succinctly: 'Ideology is something that obscures while making you believe that nothing is obstructed or hidden.' This answer made a deep impression on me and still resonates with me today. In many ways, Professor Dai has been a lifelong role model for me, embodying the ideals of intellectual pursuit and the possibilities of being a woman scholar.

To the spirit of Chinese rock – *Yaogun* – thank you. However subjective it is, its impact on me – marked by raw authenticity, sincerity, passion, and defiance – has been a constant, if quiet, presence. This energy I experienced in Beijing's underground scenes over two decades ago carried me through years of displacement, grounding me even as I drifted between cultural peripheries. It taught me to question, to resist, and to find home and belonging in dissonance.

I would like to thank Lived Places Publishing and all its members. Lived Places appeared at a pivotal time – after a global pandemic and a long period of isolation and quarantine – when I began to question many aspects of the academic publishing system itself. It emerged as a bright light in an otherwise grey and confusing atmosphere, giving me the courage and motivation to merge dissertation and memoir, and to integrate my lived experiences in various places with academic inquiry. I am particularly grateful to David Parker, co-founder of Lived Places, for his vision, principles, and commitment to a publishing project that broadens the scope of traditional academic disciplines and provides a platform for many underrepresented and previously unheard yet valuable voices. Without the emergence of publishers like Lived Places, this project would probably not have found its place on library shelves.

My heartfelt gratitude to Nila Ginger Hofman and Janise Hurtig, editors of the *Cultural Anthropology* collection, for accepting the proposal for this book and including it in their series. Their encouragement and vision came at a crucial moment when I was uncertain about how to approach the realisation of such a project. It was their suggestion to adopt autoethnography as a method that offered me the inspiration and clarity I needed to convey the messages within this work. Throughout the writing process, they have been unwaveringly supportive, dedicating their time and expertise to reading, editing, and providing insightful and thoughtful feedback. Their anthropological and musical insights, their values, and their professional integrity have been invaluable to me, and I am deeply appreciative of their generosity and care. This work would not have been possible without their steadfast support and encouragement, and I thank them sincerely from the bottom of my heart.

A big thank you to my friends near and far in different places around the world: Zhou Chunxi 周纯曦, Chai Xiaobei 柴晓蓓, Song Yalan 宋雅兰, Cheng Rui 程蕊, Liang Hongling 梁宏

玲，Rachel Huang 黄蕊, Chan Kit 阿杰, Rajohn Ali, Zora Lee, Bob and Sylvie, Rose, Laetitia, Françoise, Chi, Erwan, Jean-David, Laure, Kakuko, Lionel, Pauline, Fred, Antonio, Shwan, Barbara, Nelson, Lucy, and Ed Saul, who took the time to listen to me and found subtle, thoughtful ways to offer their encouragement and support. I am equally grateful to the many other friends, students, and 'anonymous strangers' I have met over the years who have shared moments of vulnerability or compassion with me. Their support has come in invisible ways, often without them realising how much it means to me. I would also like to thank Poppy, my cat, who has been a constant presence, a true family member, and a stable source of emotional support. Each of them, in their own way, shared precious moments with me during my years of living and researching in France and the United Kingdom, far from my family. Without their company and care, this journey would not have had the same meaning. I truly appreciate their presence in my life.

My heartfelt thanks go to my flamenco dance group (Achilipus!) and to the swing/blues dance communities (Mersey Swing and Dockside Blues) in Liverpool. Dancing with them became an essential remedy and a source of joy, offering a much-needed counterbalance to the intellectual fatigue, emotional turbulence, and daily weariness encountered throughout the making of this book. Their companionship and vibrant energy accompanied me every step of the way.

My deepest gratitude goes to my parents, whose support has sustained me throughout a journey that, for Chinese parents, may have seemed unconventional and uncertain. I am thankful for the trust and precious freedom they have given me. Despite occasional conflicts and disagreements, their presence has been a constant source of strength. In particular, I would like to thank my maternal grandmother, my mother, and my aunts, whose personalities and ways of being have always inspired and encouraged me. This work is for the women of my lineage – their resilience lives in these pages.

Special thanks are also due to the 'Dandelion Plan' of the multicultural transdisciplinary training programme, which I participated in during the realisation of this book. I am grateful to all the mentors, tutors, and fellow participants who shared this journey of growth and exploration with me. I am grateful to Fang Man 方曼, the initiator of the Dandelion Plan, whom I first met at the Seahorse Planet podcast (China's first feminist podcast 海马星球) gathering in Berlin in 2023. The gathering itself – and meeting Man – was both empowering and a reminder that my experience of living as an 'Other' standing in between, within patriarchal structures, and my journey towards cross-cultural identity integration, was neither isolated nor in vain. Fang Man's words 'If being in-between is a destiny, then make the cracks an oasis' resonate deeply with me.

At various stages during the realisation of this work, a fundamental question kept coming up: 'At the end of the day, does any of this actually matter and make sense?' 'Is Chinese rock music – and my personal life journey – really worth all this time and effort to write about? Would anything be different if these stories remained untold?'

These doubts mirrored the existential crises I had experienced while writing my dissertation. Once again, I found solace and renewed motivation in the teachings of the Buddha (Siddhartha Gautama), who, more than 2,500 years ago, offered the profound wisdom: 'Life is not a problem to be solved, but a reality to be experienced.'

Maybe this is where the sense is: the enduring commitment, spanning nearly two decades, to exploring Chinese rock and the complicated questions of my own identity. The persistence – the irresistible impulse – to return to these themes, even after countless temptations to abandon them, has become a defining thread in the fabric of my existence. I have come to realise that the true meaning of such work lies not in its final product or conclusions but in the journey itself: the permission to get lost and find oneself again; the ambiguity that exists between meaning and non-meaning; the unforeseen perspectives that arise from constant questioning. These experiences weave together into a tapestry of contradiction and richness.

Through years of research, reflection, and writing, as well as periods that I once dismissed as 'lost' or 'dead', I have come to believe that it is this intertwined, contradictory, and unpredictable process that defines my way of being in the world. Embracing this awareness has transformed the whole endeavour into an unforgettable odyssey – imbued with the liberating joy that can be found even in the most uncertain, the most difficult moments.

I am deeply grateful for this discovery and wish to share it with all who might find resonance in it. Ultimately, this work is a tribute to the infinite wisdom and compassion that silently permeate the universe.

Learning objectives

- Critically explore Chinese rock music as a cultural lens for understanding China's socio-political transformation and its entanglement with global power dynamics in the post-reform era.
- Understand the relationship between self-perception and social/structural conditioning. Learn to interrogate how a persistent, solid, independent, yet ultimately illusory selfhood is constantly forged through intersecting cultural, historical, and geopolitical forces, using autoethnography as a method of inquiry.
- Analyse the dynamic interplay between artistic innovation, ideological constraints, and market commodification in shaping cultural production, authenticity, and resistance.
- Investigate how transnational movement and cross-cultural encounters challenge fixed notions of self, otherness, and belonging.
- Reflect on how knowledge and media production can both contest and reinforce power asymmetries, shaping narratives of authenticity and influencing whose voices are heard in global discourse.
- Develop an understanding of how reflective engagement with personal experience in cultural exploration can foster intellectual, emotional, and spiritual transformation.

Introduction

This book traces the evolution of Chinese rock music – from its rebellious emergence in the late 1980s to its complex and often invisible/contradictory role in today's global cultural landscape. But it is not just a story about music. As I argue throughout this work, Chinese rock music is deeply implicated in the broader social transformations that have shaped contemporary China, particularly in the wake of the reform and opening period that followed the Cultural Revolution.

Through key historical moments, I explore how Chinese rock music evolved from an authentic, defiant expression of individual and collective yearning for greater freedom and openness into a cultural product increasingly shaped – and at times constrained – by market forces and consumerist ideologies. This transformation paralleled China's accelerated transition to a state-led, market- and technology-driven economy in the twenty-first century, illuminating the tensions between cultural resistance, ideological restriction, and commodification.

More than a chronicle of musical history, this book examines China's profound social metamorphoses over the past few decades. It traces how the evolution of rock music has mirrored the nation's changing identity, as it navigates a complex path from its revolutionary past to its aspirations to become a prosperous and powerful modern socialist state, while simultaneously embracing a market economy. In this light, the history of Chinese rock becomes a lens through which to examine the dynamic interplay between artistic expression and ideological restriction, between countercultural authenticity and commercial influence. It also offers insight into the contested and evolving discourse of national identity within an increasingly globalised power structure.

At its core, this work is as much a personal journey as it is an academic inquiry. Since childhood, I have been haunted by questions that seem both intimate and universal: What makes me who I am? Ultimately, who am I? As a lifelong fan of rock and alternative music, these questions naturally converged with my academic and emotional engagement with Chinese rock music – its history, its cultural meanings, and its power to shape individual and collective self-perceptions.

Leaving China and living in different cultural and social landscapes in France and the United Kingdom over the past two decades has added new layers of complexity to my reflections on identity. My experiences abroad have often challenged the assumptions I once held about Europe and the West, forcing me to rethink not only the myths of the 'Other', but also those embedded in my own upbringing and cultural conditioning. Gradually, I came to realise that my sense of self was not only rooted in my Chinese heritage, but was also deeply influenced by transcultural currents that transcended national boundaries. Growing up in post-reform China, my identity has been constantly shaped by global power dynamics, historical legacies, and ideological undercurrents – forces that work quietly but decisively to shape how I see myself and the world.

This book, then, does not simply analyse Chinese rock music as an object of study; it links its cultural evolution to my own search for integration between research and lived experience. It is both an academic exploration and a personal narrative and introspection – one that interweaves music, society, and the unfolding journey of self-understanding.

Throughout, I argue that personal introspection is never an isolated act – it is always mediated by broader cultural, socio-political, and structural conditions and is influenced by deep-rooted power dynamics. As I reflect on my own evolving sense of identity, I also examine how the trajectory of Chinese rock reveals enduring tensions: between individual expression and collective belonging, between ideological constraints and creative resistance, between authenticity and commodification, between rebellion and assimilation. Beyond China's internal socio-political currents, I also argue that this trajectory cannot be disentangled from global dynamics shaped by Western hegemony, cultural imperialism, and the lingering shadows of colonial history.

In this way, *Interrogating Chinese Rock* becomes more than a study of music. It is a deeper examination of how cultural and personal identity is constantly shaped, challenged, and renegotiated within shifting landscapes of power, ideology, and global interconnectedness.

Prelude

My encounter with rock 'n' roll in the People's Republic of China – A call for self-awareness

Is rock music still holding its ground in the contemporary soundscape? In an age where many struggle to commit to entire albums with repeated lyric immersion, the cultural discourse and urban nightlife scene have pivoted towards indie, lo-fi, electronic, instrumental, atmospheric, and dance music. The heyday of alternative rock and folk, with their emblematic calls for universal love, wider justice, or those progressive eight-minute guitar riffs, seems to have waned. The rebellious labels and sociopolitical undertones once synonymous with rock appear to be dissipating in the digital era, largely influenced by the rise of tailored consumer-oriented, highly personalised listening experiences, and streaming platforms.

In our era of constant information flow and fast-paced living, it's understandable that many find it challenging to sustain focus and patience. Instead of immersing themselves in entire albums, people are inclined to buy singles or individual songs, especially those with succinct lyrics that demand minimal scrutiny, navigating the rapidly evolving musical landscape. Presently, rock music no longer serves as the primary symbol of musical expression delving into raw emotions 'from the guts', a role that has shifted largely towards genres like rap. It no longer stands as a force challenging established orders or the status quo, nor is it perceived as a dedicated vehicle for activism promoting collective justice, peace, and freedom, however subjective these concepts may be.

Nevertheless, my initial encounter with Chinese rock music as a 14-year-old eighth-grade student in 1997 in the city of Kunming (capital city of the Yunnan Province, in the southwest of China) surely played a pivotal and significant role for me. It not only awakened my individual subjectivity but also sparked my curiosity to question the broader social structures and mechanisms in which I was embedded and conditioned.

I was a diligent student who always achieved excellent grades at school, earning praise and being viewed as a 'role model' by teachers and other adults. I was also a dutiful daughter, always comporting myself as a respectful junior for my parents and their acquaintances, conforming to societal expectations and Chinese traditional values. In the broader context of Chinese society since the 1980s, girls have often been labelled as 'nice' and 'gentle' and positioned as models of virtuous behaviour. This ideal has been consciously or subconsciously embodied in my own behaviour.

From an early age, my fascination with music was apparent. However, my musical exposure remained confined to select world-famous classic music extracts featured on national TV and radio channels, comprising traditional Chinese folk songs and the 'revolutionary tunes' ingrained in my parents' generation, echoing through our home in repetitive cycles. It wasn't until the mid-1990s, during my junior high school years, that the floodgates to the expansive realm of global popular music swung open. The transformation was facilitated by the circulation of stereo sets such as CD/VCD players and Walkmans into private households, as well as the accompanying burgeoning market for popular music. In addition, the advent of foreign TV channels – including Hong Kong and Taiwan channels and MTV – broadcasting on Chinese television and the proliferation of record shops in major cities across China contributed to my transformation.

My initiation into the world of popular music was orchestrated by my uncle, a passionate popular music amateur and university student in engineering at the time. Under his influence, I discovered a rich tapestry of popular music from Hong Kong and Taiwan. Like many of my peers in junior high, I was captivated by the allure of charismatic idols, dazzling outfits, dynamic performances, and the rhythmic beats of popular tunes from these regions. The music exuded a freshness and modernity, placing little emphasis on moral messages or aesthetic standards, but rather on expression and enjoyment. In a China marked by a strong collective mindset and strict social norms, navigating life as a teenage girl, a dutiful daughter, and a 'model student' in perfect alignment with societal expectations, this musical realm resonated intimately with my young, inquisitive heart. It provided an indirect avenue to process the inner voices and subtle feelings of individuals, which had limited space for expression at the time.

In the summer of 1997, during my last days of junior high school, a good friend lent me two tapes of *Yaogun* (摇滚; the Chinese term for rock music and a literal translation of the term 'rock'n'roll'). One was titled *Shameful Being Left Alone*, by Chinese rocker and songwriter Zhang Chu张楚, and the other was titled *N. 43 Baojiajie Road* by the Beijing-based rock band No. 43 Baojiajie Road (鲍家街43号). Initially challenging to grasp and appreciate, the melodies and lyrics weren't always smooth, often punctuated by disruptive notes and noise. The lyrics carried an obscure and sometimes 'dark' and angry tone. Yet, there was an inexplicable allure to the music, the rhythm, the sound, and the lyrics, which prompted me to listen to these songs repeatedly:[1]

> Bless these people who are ready to sell themselves,
> who are ready to get moved.
> They don't want to die, and they don't know the destination.
> 'God bless those who'd been fed well'
> 《上苍保佑吃完了饭的人民》
> (Zhang Chu 张楚)

> There's no happiness there.
> Just a big wall.
> I'm like a little bird
> Reality is a cage
> I'm like a little bird

> Flying around
> Flying around
>
> 'Little bird' 《小鸟》
> (No. 43 Baojiajie Road 鲍家街43号)

It dawned on me that this was a unique genre, evoking an entirely different set of emotions and modes of expression compared to the classic, folkloric, 'revolutionary', or Hong Kong and Taiwanese popular tunes I had encountered before. It was a bit noisy, loud, inharmonious, and cynical; yet, despite leading a seemingly normal and carefree life, I found myself resonating deeply with the raw emotions and feelings conveyed by the songs.

Reflecting on the past, it feels as though a beam of light had pierced through a superficial optimism, a societal numbness that veiled a reluctance to confront 'the shadowy side of the moon' – a comprehensive picture of the 'truth'. To me, this light carried a potency derived from an authentic commitment to truthfulness – a sincerity extended both to oneself and the mundane facets of everyday life. It involved an acknowledgement of frustration, disappointment, emptiness, and a dearth of space for personal emotions – an avenue through which one could engage with life in its raw authenticity, comprehending things as they truly are.

The policy of 'reform and opening up' （改革开放） was introduced by the Chinese leader Deng Xiaoping 邓小平 in the late 1970s following the death of Mao Zedong. It is best known for introducing elements of a market economy into what had previously been a rigidly planned system. 'Reform and opening up' marked a clear departure from the Cultural Revolution and Mao

Zedong's totalitarian regime, and Deng played an important role in developing the concept and practice of 'socialism with Chinese characteristics'. Therefore, in the context of the reform and opening-up policies that characterised China in the 1990s, a period in which the population was primarily concerned with securing three meals a day and seeking opportunities for a more prosperous life, these two *Yaogun* tapes represented a personal pivotal juncture. For the first time, through music, I was in touch with alternative individual voices and authentic experiences. Only in retrospect did I realise that this encounter with rock 'n' roll served as a call to self-awareness and a portal through which I could express the personal frustrations and pressures I had been carrying for years as a 'model student' and 'good girl'. It also sparked my curiosity to look around me and begin to examine the structural influences that shaped my personal sense of identity and perceptions. These structural influences had several facets: from the cultural significance of rock music as a global phenomenon, to the unique identity and ideology about the rebellious spirit of Chinese rock, to the broader context of Chinese society during the reform era of the 1990s. Together, these forces not only shaped my understanding of popular music but also revealed how deeply my sense of identity and worldview were intertwined with the cultural and social changes of the time.

I can now assert that my present self-perception would not have taken shape without my encounter with *Yaogun* and immersion into the realm of rock in the following years. It is only in recent years that I've come to truly appreciate the profound impact rock music has had on my life – both as an individual and as a Chinese woman.

In my academic exploration as well as in this book, I embarked on a journey to delve into the history, ideology, and pivotal moments shaping Chinese rock music. This genre is intricately intertwined with China's modernisation and social transitions following the reform and opening-up policy. Examined through this lens, Chinese rock serves as a microcosm for understanding the ongoing 'identity searching' voyage of a modern China.

PART I
Understanding Chinese rock, or *Yaogun*: A sociopolitical history and metaphor for 'identity searching'

In the annals of Chinese history, rock made its entrance at a pivotal moment – the onset of the sweeping narrative of the '30 years of reform and opening up' orchestrated by the Chinese authorities. This momentous period unfolded just after the conclusion of the Cultural Revolution, which was instigated by Mao

Zedong, and marked the dawn of Deng Xiaoping's economic change, characterised as 'capitalism under socialist state control'. From its inception, Chinese rock has been intricately interwoven with the formation of a 'new socialist China' – aligning itself with the 'nation-state' model and contributing to the overarching narrative of 'modernity'. Gregory Lee emphasises that 'Chinese modernisation' adheres to a historical endeavour of reconstructing or constructing China, drawing parallels to the Western 'nation-state' model:

> Until the middle of the twentieth century in Chinese, 'modernisation' was called 'westernisation', the West was synonymous with modernisation. In this sense, to a large extent the China we see today is the result, the 'success' of a century-old project: the reconstruction of China, or rather the construction of China, because a century ago China as a modern nation-state after the fall of the Soviet Union was still in its infancy. After the collapse of the Empire and the Manchu Qing dynasty, the country was still to be created. (Lee, 2012a: 35)

In this sense, the concept of rock, introduced into China from the West in the 1980s, exemplifies a form of acculturation, playing a significant role in shaping the narrative of modern Chinese history and culture. It incorporates diverse musical frameworks from its Western counterparts, sharply diverging from both 'ancient China' and the era of 'revolutionary China'. This divergence encompasses various elements, spanning from form to content: sound and rhythm, musical instruments, production technology, a pronounced emphasis on individual voice, and an 'unconventional, independent spirit', unfamiliar and unwelcome to the collectivist mindset. In essence, Chinese rock embodies the concept of 'modernity' as China endeavours to establish a new identity as a 'modern nation-state with socialist characteristics' in the era of globalisation.

Nevertheless, despite its indisputable presence in Chinese society since the 1980s, Chinese rock music remains largely unfamiliar or unknown to the broader global audience. The scarcity of Chinese rock on prominent music streaming platforms nowadays, such as Spotify or Apple Music, mirrors the obscured depiction of a culturally modernised China in mainstream media or literature outside of China. Often, this depiction focuses solely on the narrative of 'China's Miracle' within the economic domain. So, if Chinese rock indeed exists, various questions arise: what institutions underpin its existence and maintenance, and for whom does it exist? Why has Chinese rock not been able to permeate and disrupt the narrative of Chinese modern history and resonate on a broader scale, like the social movements closely associated with rock music in the 1960s in the United States, Great Britain, or later in Eastern Europe? If Chinese rock is noticeably absent from the global music scene today, what could be the possible causes? Numerous questions abound, yet there are no definitive answers. It is with this multitude of questions, both from a social and personal perspective, that I embarked on my journey to interrogate Chinese rock in a PhD project in France.

This journey began many years after my initial encounter with rock in Kunming and after countless memorable gigs and nights as a rock fan during my university years in Beijing. It was only upon leaving China, studying, and residing in France and then the United Kingdom for nearly two decades, that I began to realise my motivation to inquire into Chinese rock extends beyond mere curiosity about Chinese society and history. It is inexorably linked to my own personal identity, my sense of belonging, and my position in the world.

Inevitably, my investigation into Chinese rock, or *Yaogun*, prompts me to contemplate not only the global landscape of rock music but also the complex dynamics of the political economy of rock. Throughout my research, I've observed a significant disparity between Western and Chinese perspectives on rock music in general. Prior to this personal epiphany, I held an idealised notion of rock as universally absolute – a notion akin to the ideals of 'modernity' and 'progress' propagated by Chinese media and intellectual elites since the 1980s. Thus, this book is not only an exploration of the origins of the ideology of rock but also an attempt to address the differences in perceptions of rock music between these two different worlds: China and the West (mainly US-European societies).

During my exploration of rock's impact on Chinese society, I diverged from the traditional rock hubs of the United States and the United Kingdom. This journey not only revealed differing perceptions of rock but also led to a profound shift in my own identity. Formerly rooted in a singular cultural identity tied to my upbringing and social environment, I experienced a gradual evolution towards a more diverse and integrated sense of self throughout the years.

In an era marked by unprecedented mobility and transnational living, how is one to understand the connection between self-perception, sense of belonging, cultural identity, and the ever-changing, heterogeneous societal environments? Is there potential to bridge personal introspection with societal liberation? The latter part of this book reflects on my journey of identity integration, navigating these complex questions along the way.

1
The rise of Chinese rock: A vessel for collective aspirations and echoes of individual liberation

'Chinese rock', 'rock in China', or *Yaogun*? – Defining identity: The naming conundrum of Chinese rock music

As both a listener and researcher of Chinese rock, I constantly grapple with how to define this phenomenon – should it be called 'Chinese rock', 'rock in China', or '*Yaogun*'? The choice of name carries significance. Naming a group or a cultural form is never a neutral act; it often reflects power structures, especially for individuals or groups operating within an established hierarchy.

In the case of rock music, the dominant terminology and classification of styles have been shaped by the mass media in the United States and Europe and have been well received worldwide before arriving in China, creating a Western-centric framework. This means that rock music from other parts of the world is often judged by these pre-existing standards, raising questions of legitimacy and authenticity. As a result, both musicians and scholars of rock must navigate this imbalance, challenging or even deconstructing these inherited labels to make space for diverse expressions of rock beyond the Western canon.

Originating during the Cold War era, the terms 'First World' and 'Third World' delineate countries based on their socio-economic and political systems, with the former encompassing capitalist democracies. The label 'Third World' emerged within the context of the three-world model, signifying nations outside the capitalist 'First World' and the communist 'Second World'.

While the term 'rock' is widely acknowledged as a descriptor for the musical movement originating in the 1950s in the United States, discourse surrounding its counterparts in other regions, particularly in the 'Third World', has been more intricate. The label 'Chinese rock' has gained prevalence in popular media and academic literature as the designated term for depicting the phenomenon of rock music in China. Conversely, names of similar musical movements in the 'First World' tend to be less standardised, often linked to specific nationalities. Terms such as 'American rock', 'English rock', 'German rock', 'Canadian rock', or 'French rock' are infrequently employed.

The selection of words, whether intentional or subconscious, inherently implies an ideological framework rather than a concrete reality. As discussed earlier, the emergence and evolution of rock in China since the early 1980s are intricately connected to the historical endeavour of constructing a 'modern Chinese nation-state'. Rock, serving as a representative of 'modern music', perfectly embodies the concept of 'modernity' with its roots in the Western 'cradle', whether real or perceived. Since the early 1980s, China has witnessed significant political and economic reforms marked by the country's reform and opening-up policies. Intellectual discourse was evolving, prompting a reassessment of China's historical and cultural identity. Despite China's extensive history of engagement with various intellectual traditions – including its own, Confucian, and Marxist thought – debates predominantly revolved around the impact of Western ideas and culture on the Chinese intellectual realm in the 1980s. Intellectuals engaged in discussions concerning the merits and challenges of integrating Western values, concepts, philosophies, art, and literature into Chinese intellectual discourse and cultural practices. These discussions were part of a larger dialogue about the global exchange of ideas to 'modernise China', where in fact the term 'global' exclusively referred to European perspectives, values, and achievements during that period. On this matter, Chinese scholar Dai Jinhua 戴锦华 has stated thus:

> The crucial element in the entire cultural history of modern China manifests as a successful process wherein European culture since the Renaissance and the Enlightenment gradually becomes ingrained in the

construction and imaginative 'self' of Chinese intellectuals. (Dai, 2006: 153–158)

On a broader scale, the concept of 'modernity', including 'modern music', has primarily been influenced by Eurocentric perspectives derived from the contributions of European artists, philosophers, and scholars since the Enlightenment era. This influence continues to prevail in today's global knowledge and aesthetic sphere.

For that reason, in the Chinese context, the term 'rock' specifically refers to 'Western rock' (and rock from Britain and the United States), which is recognised as the origin or centre of this musical and cultural phenomenon, possessing inherent legitimacy and authenticity. Chinese rock musicians not only feel compelled to embrace the entire myth surrounding rock but also bear the burden of being labelled a 'counterfeit' version of 'authentic rock' (despite global mutual inspiration among musicians, a British or American rock musician would rarely face accusations of being a 'counterfeit' version of an African musician). This pressure engenders persistent anxiety and complexity regarding the 'authenticity of Chinese rock' or its 'Chinese characteristics'. In fact, the rock myth, since its inception, has been coloured by alleged supremacy, prompting inquiries into why discussions about the 'American characteristic' of rock in the United States are infrequent.

In both the title and the entirety of this book, I use the term 'Chinese rock' as an equivalent to *Yaogun* for the sake of clarity and writing coherence. However, it is essential to recognise the challenge inherent in affirming one's cultural identity when selecting a designation to represent itself. This challenge is particularly pronounced in the context of Chinese rock, a music phenomenon predominantly 'imported' from the West, employing the musical language or terms from presumed 'centres of creation'.

In essence, the challenge of asserting one's identity becomes more apparent when individuals or groups on the periphery strive to define themselves using language, terms, or concepts derived from the established 'centre', which often involves navigating through layers of power structures that control and influence narratives, thereby leading to a sense of inferiority for those without the same legacy.

Cui Jian and *Rock 'N' Roll on the New Long March*: Against the odds at a historical turn

Chinese rock music has a multifaceted and complex history that reflects the country's cultural, social, and political transformations since the conclusion of the Mao era. Unlike the genesis of rock in the United States, Chinese rock emerged in the 1980s as a response to socio-political shifts in China rather than as a cultural commodity within the entertainment industry, considering the absence of private cultural companies or entertainment industries in mainland China before the late 1990s.

Cui Jian 崔健 is widely recognised as the pioneer of Chinese rock music and acknowledged as the 'godfather of Chinese rock'. Like his contemporaries, Cui Jian also hails from a family entrenched in a military background. Both his parents were professional artists affiliated with local 'cultural troupes', which were closely aligned with the Chinese Communist Party's (CCP) endeavours to disseminate its ideology and regulate cultural expression during the 1960s. Cui Jian began his professional music career at the age of 20 as a trumpet player with the renowned Beijing Song and Dance Orchestra. However, he quickly resigned from the orchestra to pursue a career as an independent artist. His musical journey started in the mid-1980s, as he played in bands with members from China and other countries, experimenting with various musical genres.

In 1986, Cui Jian performed his song 'Nothing to My Name' 《一无所有》 during a nationally televised concert in honour of the 'International Year of Peace 1986' at the Workers Stadium in Beijing (北京工人体育场). The song adeptly blended Chinese folk melodies and traditional instruments with rock and roll rhythms. It featured lyrics with abstract queries, through which Cui Jian introduced rock elements to a broad audience. This ground-breaking performance, the first of its kind on Chinese national television, symbolically marked the beginning of rock music in China.

> I once asked endlessly, when will you walk with me?
> But you always laughed at me for having nothing to my name
> I want to give you my aspirations and my freedom
> But you always laughed at me for having nothing to offer
> Oh, when will you walk with me?
> ……
> Why do you always laugh as if it's not enough?

> Why do I always have to pursue?
> Is it that in front of you, I am forever left with
>   nothing to my name
> Oh, when will you walk with me?
> Oh, when will you walk with me?[2]
>
> 'Nothing to My Name' 《一无所有》
> (Cui Jian 崔健)

In 1987, Cui Jian, assisted by the Beijing-based band ADO, released his debut album titled *Rock 'N' Roll on the New Long March* (新长征路上的摇滚),[3] featuring the hit song 'Nothing to My Name'. Between 1987 and 1988, Cui Jian and his band performed and captivated audiences at prominent Beijing universities such as Peking University, Northern Jiaotong University, Beijing Film Academy, and the Central Academy of Fine Arts, creating a sensation in the city. Cui Jian's call for renewed personal freedom and political consciousness resonated with the concerns of students and Chinese intellectuals at the time, reaching its peak where 'Nothing to My Name' 《一无所有》 became an anthem for the youth during the 1989 Tiananmen Square protests.[4]

The aftermath of the Tiananmen Square incident led to increased government scrutiny. Nonetheless, despite facing occasional censorship, Cui Jian's influence continued to grow. In March and April of 1990, Cui Jian and the band ADO initiated the 'Rock 'N' Roll on the New Long March' tour in several major cities around China with the goal of raising funds for the Asian Games (亚运会).[5] The tour was cancelled midway, but Cui Jian's influence continued to grow, leaving a lasting impact on the rock music scene in mainland China.

In 1991, Cui Jian released his second solo album, *The Solution* (解决), featuring several songs he composed prior to 1989. With a persistent exploration of new sounds, Cui Jian and his band embarked on the tour titled 'Rock 'N' Roll on the New Long March' again, traveling to major cities nationwide over the next few years. This tour ignited excitement among local youth, generating substantial enthusiasm wherever he performed. In a way, this also laid the foundation for the thriving rock music scene in Beijing during the first half of the 1990s.

In June 1992, Cui Jian organised a concert in my hometown of Kunming to support the 'cultural and educational endeavours' of Yunnan's ethnic groups. At the time, I was a nine-year-old schoolgirl who had never been exposed to rock music and was unaware of the 1989 Tiananmen Square incident. Cui Jian was just a name vaguely mentioned on TV and in the press, but I still remember adults swapping details about the concert after dinner: 'Did you hear that the chairs in the stadium were smashed by excited young people after Cui Jian's concert?'

The nationwide influence came at a cost, with Cui Jian facing media restrictions and bans on large-scale public performances by the Chinese state for 13 years beginning in 1990. Consequently, Cui Jian was considered an icon of 'anti-power' or 'fighter for democracy' by many Western journalists, especially following the 1989 Tiananmen Square incident. However, this viewpoint and narrative are limited by Cold War-era perspectives, which tend to simplify complex political and cultural dynamics into a binary contrast between the 'liberal and democratic capitalist world' (United States) and the 'totalitarian and tyrannical communist world' (Soviet Union and China). Such a view reduces Cui Jian's artistic expression and socio-political significance to a Western-centric framework of resistance, overlooking the nuanced realities of his music, personal stance, and the evolving Chinese socio-political landscape. It therefore calls for a more nuanced analysis. In fact, even during the period of media restrictions, Cui Jian managed to freely record and distribute his music and continued touring in several Chinese cities. In more in-depth conversations with Chinese scholars, Cui Jian expressed that his work delves beyond political matters, centring on fundamental individual freedoms and overcoming limitations in a fundamental sense. He underscored the simplicity of challenging political or ideological limits, framing it as a game or entertainment. According to Cui Jian, the true challenge arises when facing disapproval from close friends or loved ones who once supported you.[6]

Apart from political pressure, China's intellectual youth in the late 1980s were also under the pressure of a dogmatic collectivism that was a product of both the Cultural Revolution and the 'thousand-year tradition', functioning as a collective social norm. According to different scholars and Chinese intellectuals at the time, the emergence of Cui Jian and the message carried in his songs, along with the direct impact of the rhythms and beats of rock, inspired a certain awakening in the form of individual heroism among Chinese youth (Zha, 2006).[7] To some extent, we can argue that this awakening, stimulated by Cui Jian's rock music, has also liberated personal emotions and thought, sentiments largely unfamiliar to Chinese youth growing up under the Cultural Revolution's political pressures and bound by the collective way of thinking. Meanwhile, it has laid the basis for the growing individual awareness of the Chinese youth, which is closely linked to the notions of modernity and consumerist individualism under the influence of Western values during the 1990s and in the years that followed.

It is necessary to point out that the rise of Cui Jian and his rock music in the late 1980s in China had nothing to do with the emergence of rock as a musical genre in the West. As a matter of fact, in the 1980s and early 1990s, the popular music industry was underdeveloped in China, due both to the country's political restrictions and the music industry's rustic infrastructure – audiences lacked the financial capacity to purchase music equipment (CD players, Walkmans, etc.), and there were very limited popular music resources available on the market. Consequently, for the 1980s Chinese youth audience, rock music was more an ideology – the so-called 'rock spirit' (摇滚精神). It is contrary to the commodification of popular culture supported by different economic organisations (record companies and shops, live venues, pubs, media, streaming platforms, etc.) in which audiences get involved as consumers by nature. In short, this 'rock spirit' was highly idealistic, and largely tinted by a collective imagination of young intellectuals about the 'revolution' or 'rebellion' against the established order or the status quo – both in terms of the politics and the way of thinking at that time.

Cui Jian's performance at Tiananmen Square in 1989 aligned with the spirit of rock against the established order, resonating with the collective mindset of Chinese intellectual youth from the revolutionary era. However, the social-political environment and individual subjectivity changed considerably after the student protests in China. Finally, and as scholar Andreas Steen has summarised, 'whereas the Long March had liberated China, the New Long March would liberate the economy, and rock music would liberate the Chinese individual' (2011: 133).

In the following decade of the 1990s, China's social and economic transformation not only prepared Chinese youth to embrace a free market with endless consumer choices, but it also helped rock music integrate into the broader popular music industry as a cultural product with a certain commodity value. Chinese rock as a 'rebellious spirit' that challenged the social and political norms would slowly fade away and dissolve into a 'fashionable coolness' in the new century. However, Chinese rock did not fully enter the sphere of 'globalised mass culture' until the late 1990s. A key moment came in December 1997, when Shen Lihui 沈黎晖, lead singer of the Chinese band Sober (清醒), founded the company Modern Sky (摩登天空) in Beijing, which would become the most influential private music company in China. This development coincided with the rapid expansion of the internet in China, further accelerating the integration of Chinese rock into the global cultural network.[8]

As I have shown, Cui Jian's impact extends beyond his music, playing a crucial role in shaping China's cultural landscape during a transformative era. Over the years, he has become an iconic figure and a myth, subject to multiple interpretations and misreading, celebrated or criticised for both his musical contributions and his symbolic representation of rebellion and individual liberation in Chinese rock history. This is reminiscent of figures like Mao Zedong or Che Guevara in the broader global context of 'revolution', whether the symbolic representation is substantial or consumerist.

In sum, Cui Jian's journey epitomises the intricate interplay between socio-political dynamics and individual expression. Emerging from a family entrenched in the cultural apparatus of the CCP, Cui Jian's divergence from the established order symbolises a broader quest for identity in post-reform China. His decision to carve an independent path mirrors the collective aspirations for liberation and self-discovery within a rapidly changing societal landscape. Through his music, Cui Jian becomes a vessel for collective aspirations and echoes of individual liberation, embodying the evolving narrative of a nation grappling with its past while navigating the complexities of modernity. As the book delves into the socio-political history of Chinese rock, it intertwines Cui Jian's journey with broader themes of the search for identity, cultural evolution, and the potential for personal introspection to catalyse societal liberation. Thus, Cui Jian's cultural, symbolic, and material impact resonates far beyond the realm of music, serving as a lens through which to explore the multifaceted nuances of contemporary Chinese society.

2
Constructing myth: Revolutionary narrative of rock

> Myth is a system of communication, it is a message, and it is a form. ... Myth is not defined by the object of its message, but by the way in which it is expressed: there are formal limits to myth, there are no substantial ones... in short, a social use that is added to the pure matter.
>
> – Roland Barthes (1957: 193–194)

In this chapter, I adopt Roland Barthes' semiotic framework to examine the myth of rock's revolutionary narrative. As Barthes argues, myth is defined not by its content but by the way in which meaning is constructed and communicated. It transforms cultural objects into ideological messages, shaping their social meaning beyond their original form. Applying this perspective, I explore how the revolutionary connotations of rock music have been shaped and repurposed through layers of cultural and social signification. The notion of 'revolutionary rock' does not exist as an absolute reality but emerges through discursive processes that frame it as a symbol of resistance, individual liberation, or even commodified rebellion. In this way, the discourse of Chinese rock in the following chapter also operates within the broader semiotic system of myth, where meanings are shaped not only by musicians and audiences but also by media and market narratives, state ideologies, and global cultural flows.

According to Yuval Noah Harari in his book *Sapiens*, the key element that unifies and creates human society is the ability to cooperate on a large scale using shared myths and narratives. Harari argues that Homo sapiens are unique among species due to their capacity to believe in and adhere to imagined realities, such as religions, ideologies, and social constructs like money and nations. These shared myths enable humans to organise in larger groups, coordinate collective actions, and establish complex social structures. Therefore, the ability to create and believe in shared fictions is crucial for the formation and cohesion of human societies throughout history (Harari, 2015).

To understand the role and impact of rock music, including Chinese rock, within various social and political structures and contexts, it is essential to analyse how the concept of rock music was created, echoing Harari's observations. This chapter examines the ideology, or myth (Barthes, 1957), or shared fiction (Harari, 2015) of rock, which was imbued with revolutionary rhetoric and deeply rooted in the global collective consciousness during the 1960s and 1970s. It unfolds in two layers: first, an examination of the origins of the rock myth in the United States and Europe, and second, its projection and adaptation two decades later in China. Through this exploration, it becomes clear that both the 'revolutionary' myth of rock and its Chinese counterpart – *Yaogun* – are consequences of interactions between social and political changes and shifting subjectivities, rather than inherent realities. Not only do they demonstrate a remarkable ability to adapt to specific socio-political contexts, but they also play crucial roles in major social movements. They are shaped by and at the same time continue to shape societal changes and collective/individual consciousness within different societal structures.

One aspect of this exploration involves debunking the myths surrounding the 'revolutionary' rhetoric associated with both rock and Chinese rock music. Originating in the 1960s in the West and persisting in China, this narrative aligns the history of Chinese rock with that of the West. The objective here is to deconstruct these myths and reveal the complex realities behind the cultural and political narratives surrounding rock and Chinese rock music. In doing so, it also exposes a global hierarchical structure in the dissemination and reception of knowledge and information in general.

Constructing the myth of rock: Creation of a 'centre'

Defining rock as a cultural phenomenon is a complex task, as interpretations vary depending on individuals' social and psychological backgrounds. What is rock? Some view rock as a musical genre that stems from the diverse influences of American popular music, while for others, it is a musical genre that mixes various sources; a specific dance; or a lifestyle and attitude! But it's also hip-swinging, rock star poses and cars, guitars, sex and drugs, screaming, romance, hours on the road, raw emotions, all-nighters on huge stages, wild audiences, and, above all, 'noise'!

Rock myth is commonly associated with rebellion and youth, conveyed through loud music, body movements, and straightforward lyrics. In addition, it is intrinsically linked to the social movements and revolutionary spirit of the 1960s. This perception of rock is widely accepted and resonates with audiences worldwide. However, it is important to consider how and why this perception has come to dominate the narrative surrounding the essential traits of rock music on a global scale. Meanwhile, for modern nation-states like the People's Republic of China (PRC), which has historically discouraged individual expression that goes against the mainstream and provided limited socialeconomic infrastructure for subcultural phenomena prior to the state-controlled market economy era, it can be difficult for such movements to thrive. Why and how do generations who grew up in mainland China during the 1970s and 1980s, with limited access to internal as well as external information and little exposure to rock 'n' roll music or major international music and television platforms, and before the emergence of the internet and algorithms, identify with and adopt to the 'rebellious' spirit of rock, including aspects of self-liberation (physical, mental, and psychological) in daily life? As someone who was born in the early 1980s in the PRC, and who had somehow internalised the system of traditional and socialist Chinese values, I found myself intrigued by the question of how the myth of rock, which seems to contradict these values, became so influential to me. This question was also the focus of my research journey.

To answer these questions, it is necessary to explore the origins of the basic concepts of rock. Understanding how these concepts are shaped, spread, and acknowledged is crucial to comprehending the rock myth and its projection in China later, as well as similar cultural narratives that are masquerading as 'common sense' or 'tradition'. Therefore, the first step in decoding the myth is to examine the ontology of rock.

Two dimensions of the ontology of rock
(a) From metaphysical and philosophical perspectives:

One way to look at rock is to see it as an embodied practice and a 'way of living'. At its core, rock represents a 'mode of human existence' that transcends specific historical, geographical, economic, and cultural contexts. It embodies some fundamental philosophical ideals around human existence and conditions, such as the principle of 'emancipation' and 'universal love', epitomised by the iconic slogan of 'Peace and Love'. This metaphysical aspect enables transcultural and comparative analyses, facilitating reflection on the metaphysics of human experience. It fosters a deep connection among musicians and enthusiasts, regardless of geographical or ideological boundaries. For instance, it is applicable in both 'socialist China' and 'capitalist America'.

(b) From anthropological, critical ethnographic, and cultural studies perspectives:

From the intersection of anthropological, critical ethnographic, and cultural studies perspectives, rock is never just a musical genre or attitude of living but a constructed myth – a symbolic system that carries ideological and socio-cultural meaning. In this chapter and the following one, I explore how this myth has been shaped, circulated, and appropriated in different social contexts, providing the theoretical ground for all discussions of rock and Chinese rock in this book.

This focus is justified by the broader observation that human societies, despite a fundamental desire for connection, are often misled and fragmented by competing ideologies and power struggles. Throughout history, conflicts rooted in race, gender, ethnicity, religion, and national identity have demonstrated how collective narratives – particularly those tied to cultural expression – can both unify and divide. Rock, as a global phenomenon, has been mythologised in ways that reflect these tensions, with its revolutionary image shifting across historical and cultural contexts.

One of the key reasons for misreading and ideological clashes lies in how language, culture, power dynamics, and media operations intertwine to shape the way we see the world. These forces don't just influence perception – they actively mould it, often in ways that go unnoticed, often deepening divides and fuelling misunderstandings. As meanings are constructed and mediated through discourse, rock's revolutionary ethos has been framed, appropriated, and reinterpreted in diverse ways. Power structures influence who gets to define rock's meaning, while media operations play a crucial role in amplifying or suppressing certain narratives. The concept of rock music is a nuanced one, shaped by diverse contexts. It could be used by authorities or other power agents in different historical and social-political contexts to convey entirely different, even opposing, messages.

When Cui Jian first performed 'Nothing to My Name' at the Workers Stadium in Beijing, Mr Rong Gaotang, the director of the National

Sports Committee who was present at the concert, angrily withdrew from the show. As a result, Cui Jian became a controversial figure. Some critics have therefore labelled Cui Jian and his rock music as an example of 'capitalist liberalism' (Zhao, 1992).

In contrast, David A. Noebel, an American evangelist, made several controversial claims about rock music and the Beatles in the 1960s and 1970s, asserting that they were part of a communist plot to corrupt American youth (Noebel, 1966), reflecting the moral panic and Cold War anxieties of the time, particularly among conservative Christian groups in the United States.

These contrasting discourses on rock music reveal contradictions within the dominant ideologies that shape each narrative, rather than inherent qualities of rock itself. They underscore the constructed and fluid nature of the rock myth, which is continually adapted to serve the ideological interests of those who propagate it.

The revolutionary rhetoric of rock myth

Rock music was not inherently associated with the rhetoric of revolution. It's commonly recognised that rock music emerged as a dynamic and diverse genre that drew from various musical traditions and cultural influences in the mid-twentieth century in the United States. Artists such as Chuck Berry and Little Richard played significant roles in shaping the early sound of rock, and Elvis Presley brought the genre to its peak. He not only did this in terms of music but also by breaking down racial barriers as a white performer who embraced and popularised African American musical styles. Elvis Presley's ascent to stardom coincided with the emergence of youth culture in the 1950s. His provocative dance moves also challenged societal norms of the time, making him a symbol of youthful rebellion and individual freedom.

However, it was not until the 1960s that the big concept of 'revolution' emerged, emphasising the social impact of rock, particularly in Britain. Popular music scholars, such as Peter Wicke, have noted the trend among popular musicians towards themes of revolution during this time. For Wicke, the shift towards the revolution rhetoric in the rock music scene was exemplified by the Beatles' album *Sgt Pepper's Lonely Hearts Club Band* in 1967 and their politically charged song 'Revolution' in 1968. Other bands, such as the Rolling Stones and Pink Floyd, also contributed to this trend during the same period. Wicke (1990) argues that this 'self-awareness' is a cultural legacy from nineteenth-century European Romanticism, which inspired British rock musicians to view themselves as artists with social responsibilities. Albums released in 1968 exhibited avant-garde characteristics, indicating increased self-consciousness among rock musicians, amid growing student activism, civil rights demonstrations, and anti-war movements, and a departure from the carefree rock and roll of the 1950s in the United States. However, despite this rhetorical shift towards revolution and political consciousness, the commercial nature of rock music remained unchanged, as the industry continued to package and market these new themes for mass consumption. In summary, during the 1960s, rock musicians emphasised skill, technique, individual expression, and political consciousness, distancing themselves from the feel-good motives of 1950s' rock in general, even as the genre remained deeply embedded within the structures of the music industry.

By the late 1960s, rock music was widely associated by the mass media with social movements and rebellious voices. It was portrayed as a symbol of rebellion and countercultural values, often used as an advocacy tool to motivate the public, challenge established norms, and promote social change. The association between rock music and rebellion spread globally, influencing youth cultures and social movements in other parts of the world. In sum, the late 1960s cemented rock music's reputation as a vehicle for social revolution and change – a legacy that continues to influence musicians and activists today. However, this association was neither uniform nor universally accepted, with its meanings and functions varying across different audiences, cultural contexts, and subgenres. While some perceive rock as a symbol of rebellion and resistance, others interpret it as a broader form of artistic expression and entertainment, serving different purposes, including commercial ambition. In addition, the rhetoric of revolution is characterised by its contradictions. Rock musicians have continually grappled with questions of authenticity and commercialism within the popular music industry. As exemplified by the Beatles, Rolling Stones, Pink Floyd, Doors, and Led Zeppelin, rock musicians have achieved significant commercial success, global fame, and substantial wealth within the very social and economic system they criticised and claimed to challenge.

Roland Barthes' theory of myth sheds light on the construct of revolutionary rhetoric surrounding the rock. According to Barthes, myth functions as a secondary system in which signs lose their original meaning and take on new associations – often the meanings constructed by dominant powers. This concept is illustrated by everyday examples such as the national flag. Initially, the flag is simply a piece of cloth with colours and patterns. However, within Barthes' mythological framework, it is transformed into a symbol of patriotism and national identity. The form of the cloth is linked to the concept of patriotism, creating a new meaning that transcends its material existence. In this process, historical and ideological dimensions disappear as meaning becomes intertwined with form. Barthes suggests that myth tends to naturalise concepts, presenting them as factual systems despite their semiological nature.

In this section, I argue that rock music in the United States and Britain in the 1960s functioned as a mythological system, similar to the concept proposed by Barthes. Melody and rhythm (the signifier), drawn from multiple sources and already rich in meaning (the signified), formed the basis of this new genre of popular music. This combination became the form of rock music, embodied by key figures in the music industry and media such as the Beatles, the Rolling Stones, and the Doors. These artists became iconic symbols of rock in the 1960s, and their images and narratives were heavily promoted through media and marketing campaigns.

At the same time, these figures became intertwined with the social movements of the era and the wider countercultural wave. Their music and personalities became increasingly associated with the rhetoric of revolution, transforming them into symbols of artistic freedom and rebellion against social norms. However, the original semantic richness of rock's melodies and rhythms, which carried a distinct heritage rooted in geographical, ethnic, and cultural influences, was gradually stripped away.

In its place emerged a new, simplified 'sign' that emphasised the genre's association with personal freedom and countercultural, revolutionary ideals. Moreover, from its inception, this new 'sign' was predominantly represented by uniformed, white, male-dominated bands whose mainstream appeal and intense mass media coverage have reinforced a narrow, homogenised vision of rock music, overshadowing the contributions of women, people of diverse ethnic backgrounds, and other underrepresented groups who have contributed to the development of this musical genre.

Finally, this connection between rock music and counterculture, revolutionary rhetoric was widely disseminated and embraced during the 1960s, profoundly shaping the global perception of rock history and culture. The mythological system of rock, as constructed through media, marketing, and cultural narratives, continues to influence how the genre is understood and celebrated today.

Romantic individualism and its influence on rock's revolutionary rhetoric

One of the ideological foundations of rock music, particularly its revolutionary rhetoric, is deeply rooted in the legacy of Romantic individualism. Emerging in nineteenth-century Europe as a reaction to Enlightenment rationalism and the rise of industrial capitalism, Romanticism emphasised artistic autonomy, personal expression, and a transcendent self – ideals that later became central to British art school education.

Works of scholars in the field of rock music, such as Peter Wicke's, have demonstrated the significant influence of artistic education on the ethos of rock musicians and its subsequent impact on the rock music scene of 1960s Britain. Indeed, British art schools played a significant role in shaping musicians' self-perception as cultural vanguards, positioning them not merely as entertainers but as artists with a profound social and ideological mission (Wicke, 1990). In a parallel manner, Howard Horne and Simon Frith (1984) have emphasised how British art schools nurtured an anti-establishment artistic identity, reinforcing the Romantic notion of musicians as visionary figures resisting capitalist conformity.

Meanwhile, the Romantic legacy found new resonance within the countercultural movements of the 1960s in the United States and Western Europe, when rock music became a vehicle for social and political expression. Influenced by the era's civil rights struggles, anti-war activism, and psychedelic experimentation, rock musicians embraced themes of rebellion, self-discovery, and transcendence – seen in figures like Jimi Hendrix, who described his music as 'cosmic' and 'ego-free' (Weller, 1969). Likewise, social theorists such as Jacques Attali (2001) viewed rock of the 1960s as a disruptive force capable of challenging dominant social structures.

The fusion of Romanticism's emphasis on self-expression with the global political and cultural upheavals of the 1960s shaped rock's identity as both an artistic and ideologically charged movement. The revolutionary rock myth, constructed through this discourse, positioned rock musicians as agents of change while simultaneously being commercialised and absorbed into the very system they sought to critique. This paradox continues to shape the global legacy of rock, influencing how musicians – whether in the West or in contexts like Chinese rock (*Yaogun*) several decades later – navigate the tension between authentic artistic expression, political restriction, economic manipulation, and cultural legitimacy.

Roland Barthes views myth as ethically problematic, as it obscures the arbitrary nature of signs and serves ideological interests in establishing unquestionable values. The revolutionary rock myth faces a similar ethical dilemma, as it oversimplifies the intricate historical, cultural, and social factors that contributed to its emergence. The consolidation of rock music's icons to mainly American and British artists or bands with the help of major popular music corporations and intensive media coverage reinforces the notion of the West, particularly the United States and Britain, as the unrivalled epicentre of the genre.

3
Unveiling the myth of *Yaogun*: A reassessment of rock's 'periphery'

Before the advent of globalisation in China, marked by its entry into the WTO in 2001, Chinese rock (*Yaogun*) shared formal similarities with rock music in the United States and Britain, yet it developed its own distinct identity, independent of the cultural connotations traditionally associated with rock music globally. As Jonathan Campbell, a scholar of Chinese rock, notes, it was impossible for rock music in China to be the same as rock music in America, Britain, Russia, or Japan. Indeed, until the beginning of the new millennium, social and technological advances had not yet fully freed Chinese citizens from many constraints. Prior to this period, most Chinese had little to no direct contact with foreign cultures, let alone the opportunity to absorb and integrate them (Campbell, 2011).

Prehistory: The emergence of 'modern music' in China

The emergence of Chinese rock did not occur in isolation from the broader cultural landscape of China. In fact, a significant current of modernisation and orchestration in Chinese musical practices had been developing since the late nineteenth century, with the city of Shanghai playing a pivotal role during the 1930s. However, the growth of popular music in the 1930s was suspended by the Japanese invasion and the subsequent rise of patriotism among the public and within the cultural milieu. In a way, the emergence of rock and its development in the late 1980s can be seen as a continuation of the trend of modernisation and treaty-port opening to the West that began from the late nineteenth century. Therefore, to better understand Chinese rock and the myth that has been constructed around it in the 1990s, one would actually have to re-examine the whole cultural history of China in the twentieth century in general.

Brass bands were introduced to China during the late Qing Dynasty amid a broader wave of Western influence linked to modernisation. Originally used for ceremonial and religious functions in European colonies, military brass bands soon became potent symbols of imperial power. Their impressive sound and visual impact prompted local authorities—including those in China—to adopt the format and train indigenous musicians. In the aftermath of its defeat in the Opium War and the signing of a series of unequal treaties following successive military losses, China—driven by both the pressure of Western encroachment and an urgent desire to modernise—incorporated brass bands into its military reforms since the mid-nineteenth century. European bandmasters were recruited to train Chinese troops in brass, woodwind, and percussion instruments, leading to the formation of regimental ensembles. These bands introduced Western harmonic structures and instrumentation, which would later shape the curricula of China's earliest conservatories and civilian orchestras (Kaminski, J. S., 2024).

Apart from the military reformers, it was the Taiping who introduced the practice of hymn singing in a Christian religious mode during their anti-imperial revolt in the mid-nineteenth century. They directly copied these songs from European missionaries who had gone to China and introduced the choir into the churches at the time. The choir, which was introduced into schools as a modern form of education from the 1920s onwards, proved to be a highly successful educational innovation. Concurrently, a new approach to music was introduced by Chinese students returning from abroad, who combined lyrics created by young intellectuals with traditional Chinese musical forms. A new form of music, designated 'school songs and music' (*xuetang yuege* 学堂乐歌), was subsequently introduced, which served as a catalyst for the emergence of 'revolutionary songs' during the prolonged periods of warfare in the early twentieth century in China, including civil wars and the Sino-Japanese wars.

In contrast to the revolutionary trend, another form of singing emerged in the early twentieth century known as 'lyrical singing'. This was derogatorily labelled as 'pornographic singing' by the Communist Party and closely resembled Chinese folk songs from rural areas. It focused solely on themes of personal subjects such as romantic love or daily life affairs and avoided any political commentary. Following the establishment of the PRC in 1949, this apolitical genre of music was marginalised and forced into exile in regions such as Hong Kong and Taiwan. It was not until the late 1970s that this musical trend resurfaced. It is therefore notable that the call for individual voices and expressions in the advent of rock music in China during the 1980s was not only influenced by Western music and cultures following the opening-up and reform policy, but also deeply rooted in the preceding lyrical tradition that has always existed in rural areas and folkloric arts. In China, the earlier lyrical, individualised trend of the 'lyrical singing' that emerged in the Shanghai music industry during the 1920s and 1930s was already evident, although it had been constrained by the establishment of the PRC.

During the early twentieth century, China underwent a period of partial Westernisation, during which Chinese revolutionary movements embraced Western ideals such as freedom and equality. Following the decline of the Qing Dynasty and the May Fourth Movement sparked by student protests on 4 May 1919, the terms 'West' and 'Western' played a crucial role in the discourse of China's so-called renovation period, corresponding to the notion of modernisation in the early twentieth century. The May Fourth Movement is regarded as a pivotal moment in modern Chinese history, marking a rejection of traditional values and a call for social and political reform. The movement advocated for democracy, science, and nationalism, laying the groundwork for the emergence of new cultural and political movements in China. As previously stated at the outset of this section, the term 'Westernisation' was considered synonymous with 'Modernisation' in intellectual discussions throughout the mid-twentieth century in China.

However, the adoption of various Western notions and principles resulted in a paradoxical situation, as the revolutionary songs of the era – often rooted in nationalistic and anti-imperialist themes – were deeply infused with the Western orchestration and the concept of the modern nation-state. This demonstrated China's reliance on Western concepts to initiate reform while claiming to break free from Western influence. This inherent contradiction serves to illustrate the challenge of self-perception often encountered by peripheral members who draw upon central concepts to build their distinguished identities. This is also exemplified by the emergence of Chinese rock music or *Yaogun*. Furthermore, this inherent dilemma will also accompany the process of the national identity building of a 'socialist modern China' following the entire 'reform and opening up' period.

These historical factors contributed to the delayed emergence of popular music, including rock, which had to wait until the 1980s to resurface in mainland China, nearly 50 years after its initial appearance. The term 'again' used here to describe its resurgence signifies a societal disconnect with the outside world, particularly with Western countries like the United States and Great Britain, where the notion of 'popular music' was curated and perceived worldwide.

In conclusion, the emergence of Chinese popular music and *Yaogun* in the 1980s marked a pivotal moment in the country's history. It represented a departure from the recent past, which had been characterised by decades of internal political turmoil and the Cultural Revolution. At the same time, it signified a return to earlier currents of change – both a continuation of the spirit of 'revolution' that had shaped the early twentieth century and a reaction against the Communist Revolution and its ideological legacy, in particular the internal political conflicts and class struggles. This reaction was not merely political but also cultural, as both musicians and youth sought alternative modes of expression that transcended the rigid ideological frameworks of the past. This dynamic was deeply ingrained in the collective consciousness of the youth generation, following the era of Chairman Mao.

Communist ideology and the Cultural Revolution: One source of the *Yaogun* myth

The CCP always employs propaganda music to enforce and reinforce its ideology. One example is the 'model opera' (*yangbanxi* 样板戏) genre, which dominated the Chinese cultural scene during the Cultural Revolution (1965–1976). 'Model opera' can be understood as a model for the masses, encompassing not only singing and acting but also thought and guidance. This genre is a clever fusion of the traditional Chinese Peking opera with foreign musical influences, which has become established throughout China to the exclusion of any other local opera genre. Only eight 'model operas' were created during the Cultural Revolution, to which a few rare adaptations were added. For ten years, China was completely immersed in 'model opera'. It is a genre in which Western musical input is integrated and plays a significant role – at least much more important than it had been in the previous decade.

From this, it is evident that the leaders of the Communist Party were seeking to reduce the richness of 'traditional Chinese music' and make it simpler and more standardised. This also applies to the fashion of clothing. During the Cultural Revolution, the military uniform was the only acceptable form of dress for all, regardless of gender, age, or status. The military uniform thus became genuinely popular on a national scale, characterised by its monotonous shape and dark green colour. The 'godfather' of Chinese rock Cui Jian, for example, was born into a military family and was therefore familiar with military uniforms, which he later adopted as a symbol of his rock concerts, both in China and abroad.

To a certain extent, the ideology of Communism and the elements of the Cultural Revolution propagated by the CCP became an important source in the foundation of the *Yaogun* myth, which was constructed during the 1990s. Similarly, the slogan 'Peace and Love' and the hippie fashion of the 1960s and 1970s in the United States served as the 'signs and concepts' of the 'revolutionary' rock myth.

From 'variety song' to *Yaogun*: The shift towards market dynamics and individualism

The term 'variety song' translates the Chinese expression '*tongsu gequ*' (通俗歌曲), which originated in the 1930s, the initial stage of the 'modernisation' of Chinese culture. This term corresponds to the English 'popular song' and refers to the lyrical trend discussed earlier. The term 'variety song' was then merged with the term '*gangtai*' (港台), which is an abbreviation of the Chinese words for Hong Kong and Taiwan. Therefore, '*gangtai* song' literally refers to the popular songs from Hong Kong and Taiwan and was commonly used by people in mainland China in the 1980s and early 1990s.

The shift in language around 'popular song' is of great significance. It reflects not only the specific historical context of China and its relationship with Hong Kong and Taiwan between the late 1980s and early 1990s, but also an important collective social and mental shift towards the market dynamics and individualism represented by Hong Kong and Taiwan at the time. In the early 1990s, many young people in mainland China, including myself, then a junior high school student, were obsessed with '*gangtai* culture'. Various cultural phenomena from Hong Kong and Taiwan flooded the previously monotonous and dull cultural scene in mainland China, feeding the craving for fun and enjoyment of the Chinese youth, while being seen as representing a more 'developed' and cosmopolitan aspect of 'Chinese culture'. This included music, food, speech, and even architecture. Many 'Hong Kong style' restaurants popped up across the country, and in Shanghai, it even became a popular trend to put on a Cantonese accent when performing in karaoke bars. Meanwhile, many Hong Kong-English loan words were also adopted into Mandarin, such as 巴士 (Bus) and 的士 (Taxi) (Hall-Lew, 2002).

As China was experiencing a cultural deficit a decade after the end of the Cultural Revolution, it was a natural tendency for Chinese youth on the mainland to turn to the cultural products 'imported' from China's 'periphery', Hong Kong and Taiwan, which follow the market economy and had less austere political environments during the last decades, and therefore have more economic/cultural power, yet still share the same language and cultural foundation. For many years after the opening of the PRC, the mainland's music industry indeed relied heavily on its counterparts in Hong Kong and Taiwan to revive and revitalise the Chinese popular music scene across the country. As a result, these '*gangtai* songs', along with other popular music imported from the West, opposed the 'official tunes' and 'revolutionary songs' that dominated the mainstream media (mainly national television and radio channels) in the PRC, and they flourished as an independent commercial genre free from party control in the early 1990s.

The Chinese term for rock music, *Yaogun* (摇滚), first emerged in China, Hong Kong, and Taiwan in the late 1970s and early 1980s. Initially used to describe the Western musical genre of rock 'n' roll, it soon became associated with a distinctly Chinese musical style and a 'rebellious spirit'. This transformation was largely driven by iconic singers such as Cui Jian and the myth of *Yaogun* constructed by music magazines and critics in the 1990s. Consequently, *Yaogun* represented a constructed music genre imbued with an ideology that was distinct from other popular music in China, both in terms of musical style and meaning.

Deng Xiaoping's policy of reform and opening up allowed Western pop music to enter China. In the early 1980s, Chinese youth were exposed to bands and musicians such as the Beatles and Bob Dylan through radio programmes and limited, often expensive, cassettes imported by various audiovisual publishers. However, most Chinese in the 1980s had very modest incomes, and private ownership of audiovisual equipment such as telephones, televisions, and cassette or CD players was still not common. Only a privileged few could afford to buy cassettes from audiovisual shops, many of which were still state-owned. I can still remember that the first 'imported CD' that my family bought cost about 100 RMB, which was equivalent to 30–40 per cent of my mother's monthly salary in the early 1990s. Even looking at it today, it's still quite a high cost for a normal working-class household – a pricy product that's inaccessible to the majority.

Due to the scarcity of officially imported 'original' cassettes and financial constraints, many Chinese youths resorted to using white tapes to 'copy' (*fanlu* 翻录) the original tapes circulating among friends or in small circles. The concept of 'copyright' was not an issue at the time, as copyright laws were not enacted in the PRC until 1990, much later than in Europe and the United States. Therefore, the practice of copying tapes was common in the 1980s due to a lack of resources and high demand.

Consequently, the unauthorised circulation of audiovisual products, including cassettes and videotapes, emerged from coastal areas such as Guangdong Province (near Hong Kong) and flourished on the black market. The unauthorised distribution was termed *zousi* (走私) in Chinese, and it greatly influenced the development of Chinese popular music before the advent of the internet. This practice continued with the *Dakou* phenomenon, which flourished among Chinese music fans in the late 1990s and early 2000s. *Dakou* involved the importation of surplus cut-out CDs and cassettes from Western markets as plastic waste, contributing significantly to the alternative music scene. This phenomenon is discussed in greater detail in the following chapter.

It's worth mentioning that the introduction of audiovisual equipment during the reform era is also an important factor that transformed Chinese music culture. For example, the Sanyo cassette player, a famous Japanese brand of audiovisual products, became a fashion object among Chinese youth in the 1980s. Colloquially known as 'the brick', the cassette player symbolised modernity and transformed music consumption from a collective to an individual activity. This shift also marked a departure from the Mao era, when the national radio and public speakers were the only music medium. Meanwhile, the cassette player, and later the Walkman, facilitated what Castoriadis (1979: 69) called the 'privatization of the individual', allowing for personalised musical experiences and helping to shape the more individualised mindset of the next generations in China. As the Chinese popular music critic Jin Zhaojun 金兆均 has stated in his book:

> The appearance of the tape recorder in China made it possible to disseminate popular music to the masses through a personal medium, which did not depend on the centralised collective medium. The architecture of popular music was radically changed afterward. (Jin, 2002: 60)

During the initial phase of the evolution of Chinese rock music, from the mid-1980s to the late 1990s, a proper popular music industry was lacking due to the absence of a private economic infrastructure. Consequently, apart from a small number of university students who had listened to Cui Jian's music at live concerts or through the often-illicit circulation of tapes, most Chinese people had not had the opportunity to access the sonic material of rock music. Therefore, there was initially a collective imagination of what rock music is or should be before the actual listening experiences, which distinguished Chinese rock music from many other areas of the world.

In summary, my research revealed that in the early stages of Chinese rock development, the imagination and perception of rock music in the West within Chinese popular culture were largely shaped by a few limited music magazines and radio programs, and through the perspectives of some key music critics at the time.

The projection and integration of the myth of 'revolutionary' rock in China: Early rock journalism and broadcasting

Before the flourishing of pirated and *Dakou* cassettes and CDs, and before the arrival of the internet in China in the late 1990s, there was very limited media coverage of rock music. One of the main sources of information for Chinese music lovers was music magazines and certain radio programmes. Among the early media covering rock music, there were two main sources that played a fundamental role in the development of rock music in China: the music magazine *Audio&Video World* (音像世界) and a radio programme *Rock Magazine* (摇滚杂志), broadcast by the Beijing Music Channel (北京音乐台). Due to the sensitivity of the term 'rock' to the Chinese authorities, the name of the programme was later changed to *Magazine of New Music* (新音乐杂志). It was hosted by Zhang Youdai 张有待, a prominent DJ and music bar organiser based in Beijing.

Unveiling the myth of *Yaogun* 53

Figure 1: The cover of the first issue of *Audio&Video World* (October 1987). The name of the magazine was written in Chinese, English, and Japanese. Source: Wang, 王莫之 (2020a).

The *Audio&Video World* was founded in October 1987 under the CNRC (China National Records Corporation). It was the first audiovisual publication in mainland China and was instrumental in launching the first generation of Chinese rock music critics introducing Western rock music to Chinese audiences. It also hosted the first legal fan organisation in mainland China, the '*Audio&Video World* Fan Club', and was the first to hold fan meetings for singers from Hong Kong and Taiwan in Shanghai.

The '*Audio&Video World* Fan Club' began its preparations in February 1989 and was officially founded in the summer of that year. Its brochure, the first fanzine in mainland China, *Pop*

Figure 2: The cover of the *Audio&Video World* after its first redesign (March 1988 issue), which included many rock'n'roll elements.
Source: Wang王莫之 (2020b).

Music Bus, was inspired by the English name of the Hong Kong magazine *Music Bus*. At the time, legal civil society organisations were so rare in Shanghai that the fan club's registration number was 005 (Wang, 2020a). The inside cover of the first issue of the fanzine was inscribed in traditional Chinese with the names of Author and Simon, two of the main editors of *Audio&Video World* and its fanzine.[9]

> Music, for you and me, is like the water we need to survive.
> You and I are a group of fish living in the water
> Swallowing music to our heart's content

Unveiling the myth of *Yaogun*   55

Figure 3: The first fanzine in mainland China, *Pop Music Bus* No. 1, cover and inside pages. Source: Wang王莫之 (2020a).

The fan club organised regular activities for its members, highlighted by screenings of MTV and concert videos, usually held at the Community Cultural Centre for Youth in Shanghai. A distinctive feature of the fanzine was its lack of illustrations. Each issue comprised 32 pages, with participants volunteering their time and resources to handle every aspect of production, from cutting the paper to binding the pages. MTV was a rare commodity, and videotapes were provided by members with overseas connections and some foreign record companies. These tapes also helped local TV and radio stations supplement their music programming.

Initially, the fan club recruited only local members in Shanghai due to the limited seating capacity of around 500 seats. A few months later, the club began recruiting members from outside the city without any membership restrictions or separate groups; these new members were collectively known as 'associate members'. Wang Xiaofeng, one of the first associate members from Beijing, founded the Beijing chapter of the *Audio&Video World* Fan Club and appointed himself as its president. He later became one of the main authors of the influential column 'the conversation on rock'.

Among the limited media resources available in the early 1990s, two columns published in *Audio&Video World* played a fundamental role in disseminating information and knowledge about Western rock music. One column titled 'Modern Talking' (摩登谈话) introduced several albums in each issue of the magazine with reviews by the magazine's writers. The column's name was inspired by the German band Modern Talking, and its format was comparable to the disc reviews of new albums from

Europe, America, Hong Kong, and Taiwan. Interestingly, nearly a dozen writers contributed to this column – all under the pseudonym of *Audio&Video World*'s chief editor Zhang Lei 张磊 – creating the impression of a roundtable discussion with some of his understudies.

Another column entitled 'conversation on rock' (《对话摇滚乐》) played a crucial role in propagating and projecting the myth of rock to Chinese audiences. 'Conversation on rock' included a series of articles published in the *Audio&Video World* between 1992 and 1994. The two authors of 'conversation on rock', Wang Xiaofeng 王晓峰and Zhang Lei 章雷, were among the first Chinese music critics to introduce Western rock music to a Chinese audience. In addition to discussing classic rock music from the 1950s, they also introduced a variety of musical styles that were virtually non-existent in China in the early 1990s. The column included articles on Jimi Hendrix, the Beatles, and Nirvana; on early English punk rock bands (Sex Pistols, Siouxie and the Banshees); as well as on heavy metal and even grind core music. It provided a limited platform for Chinese rock enthusiasts to learn about Western rock, particularly from the United States and Britain, in a relatively systematic way. This knowledge was later supplemented by radio broadcasts and the distribution of private cassettes.

The 'conversation on rock' column offers more than just a cultural history of Western rock music; it also provides sociological and philosophical critiques from its two authors. As a result, their discussions inevitably reflect both the ideologies of rock music and their interpretations of modern capitalist society. A close reading and textual analysis of all the articles in 'conversation on rock' as

Figure 4: 'Modern Talking' section in the *Audio&Video World* page. Source: Wang 王莫之 (2020b).

part of my doctoral research shows that the authors' perspectives were shaped – consciously or unconsciously – by the broader ideologies associated with twentieth-century rock, which had already gained global recognition.

As previously discussed, the idea of 'revolution' was central to the rock myth of the 1960s. This theme was deeply rooted in nineteenth-century Romantic individualism and ideals, resonating with social movements in the United States and United Kingdom. Within the capitalist system, it was often seen as a critical response to mainstream norms. Twenty decades later, against the backdrop of China's economic and social transformation following reform and opening up, the two authors drew on the rhetoric of the rock myth to shape their arguments throughout 'conversation on rock'.

The influence of the 1960s rock myth is evident in these articles, in which the revolutionary rhetoric is juxtaposed with the socio-political environment of China 20 years later. In the inaugural column of the 'conversation on rock' in June 1992, the authors explicitly asserted that rock is not merely a musical genre, but also a cultural phenomenon and a mode of being of the 'Western youth'. They implied, however, that readers of the column might eventually 'gain insight into the essence of modern capitalist society through an understanding of rock'. To some extent, 'conversation on rock' served as an ideological foundation for the *Yaogun* myth in the 1990s, alongside the rise of Cui Jian as its most prominent symbol. To comprehend the significance of the articles in 'conversation on rock', it is necessary to categorise some extracts from the articles in this column under a few key notions. Each group of texts here will illustrate a concept, ideology, or discourse that is integral to the *Yaogun* myth in China.[10]

Rock: Inherently political, subversive, and anti-establishment

> Furthermore, to truly understand rock music, it is essential to understand the socio-cultural context behind the music. For example, why did the songs of bands such as the Sex Pistols and the Clash aim to directly criticise the capitalist system? Why did Bob Dylan's songs become the emblem of youth culture in the 1960s? And why are black people still at the forefront of fashion in the world of popular music in the United States? ('conversation on rock', June 1992)
>
> Elvis Presley has a special place in the development of rock music. As a white man, he introduced the

blues – a music of the blacks that was with the discourse of 'race' – to white listeners for the first time ... His success is because he broke the 'race' barrier in the music world and helped rock gain legitimacy in society. His influence is more interesting and appealing on a social level than on a musical level. ('conversation on rock', June 1992)

The Rolling Stones used music to 'declare war' on traditional hypocrisy, touched on a sensitive issue in society, and stimulated a rebellious mentality in young people. Their anti-establishment spirit became almost a symbol of the opposition between the underclass and the privileged class. ('conversation on rock', August 1992)

The Sex Pistols' attack on 'pop' music is an insight; it is about sex, with the aim of exposing the myth of love that lies behind sex; it is about love, with the aim of studying the family that lies behind it; it is about the family, with the aim of understanding the class system that lies behind it. Finally, it has the ultimate aim of 'exposing' the myth itself in post-war Western capitalist societies, yet 'pop' music has never addressed this. ('conversation on rock', March 1993)

Rock: Unconventional, anti-commercial (opposition of 'pop'), and representing new social consciousness

Rock in the 1960s was in some ways anti-commercial and anti-capitalist. It would be quite normal for it to be avant-garde or purely playful in the service of entertainment. It was against old tradition and old values, it created new values and new ways of living ... And why it had so many followers was because it still remains the emblem and the representation of the new culture, the new wave of thought and the new social consciousness, it still remains the spokesman of the new generation in society. ('conversation on rock', November 1992)

The avant-garde figures of the USA and European rock scene of the 1960s, of which Jim Morrison was the most representative, were lonely, desperate 'souls' who were not compatible with real society, but they never compromised. Their music was, in a way, their demands, their cries, and tears for the absolute freedom of human nature. From this point of view, they pushed rock into a much deeper and more important realm. Although the European and American rock music of the 60's is a history that cannot be reproduced, when we revisit this music today, we realize that it was the themes they brought to rock and roll that allowed the music to grow for decades and ultimately remain intact. Those cries and laments of the soul seem to be resonating again today, in this country. ('conversation on rock', February 1993)

As a true rocker, he would not compromise his art for the needs of commercialism in exchange for his art. He only wants to present and express his true feelings and thoughts through music. Rock dares to tear away all the hypocritical cover-ups and present all the truths through real eyes. ('conversation on rock', May 1993)

From the extracts presented here, it is possible to identify key concepts introduced and emphasised by the authors in 'conversation on rock', a significant column at the outset of rock music's development in China. The entire column reflects an intensified interpretation of the rock myth, with the authors placing particular emphasis on the 1960s rock movements in the United States and Britain. Naturally, their interpretations were shaped by their own cultural, social, and political contexts as well as the inevitable subjectivity of individual perspectives. Moreover, their viewpoints were further influenced by differences in time, geography, and ideology. In reading their work, I encountered both misunderstandings and idealisations of rock music, yet also a genuine aspiration to 'enlighten' the public.

The authors sought to 'transport' what they saw as rock music's 'revolutionary' and 'innovative' spirit to the socio-cultural realities of 1990s China. In doing so, 'conversation on rock' actually reinforced the dominance of American and British rock within Chinese popular culture – perhaps unintentionally – by consolidating certain musicians and bands from these regions as the unquestionable pioneers and masters of the genre. This contributed to the perception of American and British rock as the most 'authentic', while simultaneously embedding the rhetoric of revolution in their commentary and interpretations. As a result, the myth of 'revolutionary' rock was, in a sense, appropriated from the global 'centre' and introduced to Chinese audiences as a new cultural paradigm. Meanwhile, China itself was positioned – consciously or not – on the 'periphery' of the genre.

Despite these complexities, 'conversation on rock' played a crucial role in shaping the perception of rock music for a generation of young Chinese, including musicians. The column not only introduced Western rock but also contributed to the thriving popular music and *Yaogun* scene in the mid-to-late 1990s. Wang Xiaofeng, one of the authors, later co-authored *A Guide to Western*

Popular Music (欧美流行音乐指南, 2008), which became an essential reference for rock and popular music fans in China.

As well as imparting musical knowledge, 'conversation on rock' explored the cultural history of rock and its established 'revolutionary ethos', in particular rock's engagement with social issues and its subversive stance towards authority. It was clear from the articles that the writers were attempting to interpret Western society through the lens of 'revolutionary' rock and relate it to China's contemporary realities. However, the socio-political conditions of the United States and Britain in the 1960s were very different from those of China in the 1990s, making direct comparisons in popular culture difficult. Nevertheless, looking back to the 1980s, I can see certain parallels between the enthusiasm and idealism of 1960s rock and the cultural dynamism of 1980s China. Whether consciously or unconsciously, this can be seen as one explanation for the authors' emphasis on the myth of revolutionary rock.

In conclusion, the writings in the 'conversation on rock' were instrumental in shaping the imagination and perception of rock music as a revolutionary, unconventional music and culture force in China before the advent of the internet and the wider dissemination of audiovisual products throughout the country; this collective imagination of a 'revolutionary and anti-commercial' rock had in turn shaped and influenced the musical practice of many subsequent Chinese rock musicians during the 1990s.

The myth of rock portrayed through the 'conversation on rock' also helped to shape a new myth, not only as a unique Chinese modern musical genre but as an ideal artistic expression detached from power, money, and 'all the old-fashioned ways and dogmas', under the label of *Yaogun*. This new myth was embodied and catalysed by the rise of Cui Jian and reinforced in a monograph titled *Cui Jian, Screaming in the Midst of Nothing – Chinese Rock Memo* (崔健, 在一无所有中呐喊-中国摇滚备忘录) published in 1992 by Chinese music scholar and writer Zhao Jianwei 赵健伟. Just as I have demonstrated the projection of the myth of rock in China through the textual analysis of the 'conversation on rock', I have also identified some key concepts of the myth of *Yaogun* through a close reading of Zhao's book. Below are a few selected excerpts, each group of texts illustrating a concept or ideology that is anchored not only in the myth of *Yaogun* but also in the imagination of 'modernity' through the lens of a Chinese intellectual in the 1980s and early 1990s.[11]

Yaogun: A representation of cultural heroism and imaginary 'Enlightenment' – The legacy of the 'revolutionary' rock

> Since the appearance of Cui Jian and his *Yaogun*, Chinese rock has begun to take on the role of spokesman and sacrificial hero of the times, offering a means of liberation. (Zhao, 1992: 291)
>
> Cui Jian is the only famous singer in mainland China who has achieved success without relying on the official media. This is a clear revelation: as a symbol of cultural rebellion, Cui Jian's success has made rock music a cultural force in China for the first time. (Zhao, 1992: 293)
>
> In my opinion, the main reason for the total backwardness of Chinese society in modern times is not the retrogression of Chinese society itself, but the rapid progress

of Westerners since the Renaissance. It was the rapid progress brought about by the emancipation of human nature in the West since the Renaissance that left the Chinese far behind. Therefore, as I have said before, the true emancipation of a nation lies not in its independence alone, but in the human liberation and freedom of each individual in the nation. Rock stands for this sort of human liberation and freedom. (Zhao, 1992: 260)

Yaogun: An attempt at nationalism and a spiritual quest

More importantly, Cui Jian and his *Yaogun* have become the faith of a generation of young people. Although this faith has not yet received a Chinese passport, history will prove that the emancipation of human nature that this faith brings will be the national quality that China must have in order to finally modernise. China's modernisation will be the quality of its people. (Zhao, 1992: 126)
The spiritual bond that binds a nation to its soul is never broken by the interruption of space or by the circumstances of life. In the long historical process of the formation of a nation, no matter how people are displaced, they can never get rid of that 'nation complex' in the depths of their hearts and minds. For this very reason, no matter where a person goes, no matter whether he changes his nationality or not, he will never be free of this 'nation complex' in his mind. The temple of the nation will always be in the depths of his soul. (Zhao, 1992: 140)

Through the above excerpts, the characteristics of the myth of *Yaogun* are highlighted by its 'revolutionary' and 'enlightened' nature, which stands in opposition to mainstream music (pop music). This myth encompasses nationalism, cultural heroism, and a spiritual quest beyond commercial interests and market logic. Bear in mind that until the late 1990s there was no 'cultural industry' in China as there was in Britain or the United States. Instead, there was an ideology and an imagination of rock and *Yaogun*. Scholar Andrew F. Jones' comments are accurate here: 'rock has not always been about serious philosophical problems of human life. Nor are all rock singers drawn to working-class themes. Early Chinese rock was more about revolutionising musical style and image. In this context, John Lennon resembles Cui Jian more than Cui Jian resembles John Lennon' (Jones, 1992: 128). The passage reveals more about Chinese reconstructions of the nature and social function of rock than its actual form in the West, and it also reveals the essence of the myth of *Yaogun* before China entered the 'globalisation era'.

In summary, the efforts of first-generation music critics, such as Wang Xiaofeng and Zhang Lei, and the phenomenal rise of Cui Jian, which was closely linked with the student protests and social movements in the late 1980s, initially framed rock music in China as a social and artistically significant genre imbued with idealistic imagination about the 'revolution', 'subversion', and 'liberation'. During this formative period, the written word, in other words the ideal, played a pivotal role in the appropriation and dissemination of the dual myths of rock and *Yaogun*, rather than the music itself.

The dual 'revolutionary' narratives of rock and *Yaogun* myth constructed in the early 1990s were part of a wider cultural movement within Chinese popular culture in the 1990s. This period saw the establishment of consumer classes, particularly the emerging wealthy groups following the privatisation of the economy, and the development of social, cultural, and technological infrastructures in the major urban areas at an accelerated pace. To some extent, the 'revolutionary' rock music, with its serious social concerns and artistic responsibilities, resonated deeply in this context. Furthermore, the earliest *Yaogun* music, represented by Cui Jian's work and through the publications and propagation of the Chinese intelligentsia at the time, also played a pivotal role in 'enlightening the masses' at the dawn of Chinese society's journey towards a 'modern nation' and industrial modernisation. During this initial stage, Cui Jian was inevitably mythologised as a kind of 'missionary' for personal voice and freedom. This resonated with a larger collective desire for a more liberal and democratic political, social, and cultural environment, following decades of turbulence and austere political and social conditions.

Concurrently, this initial period of constructing myths around rock and *Yaogun* established the foundation for a more entertainment- and consumer-oriented rock movement that would evolve with the advent of the internet in the late 1990s. The emergence of the Modern Sky Records in 1997 and the 'New Sounds of Beijing' movement in 1999 marked a shift. These events signalled not only the end of the 1990s in Chinese modern history but also the fading of rock's 'rebellious spirit' that resonated with the Chinese youth. Till then, rock and *Yaogun* had been an expression of individual liberation, deeply intertwined with the collective consciousness, and more importantly, an ideal and aspiration for some radical social transformation, and this was not yet completely tainted by market logic and commodification pressures.

4
'China Fire' under the 'Modern Sky': Transforming Chinese society before the dawn of a new century

> To be modern is to find ourselves in an environment that promises us adventure, power, joy, growth, transformation of ourselves and the world – and, at the same time, that threatens to destroy everything we have, everything we know, everything we are.
>
> – M. Berman (1982:15)

Dreams and profits: The idealism of Chinese cultural rejuvenation with Taiwan and Hong Kong capital

In the early 1990s, the music industry in China was in its infancy, and only Cui Jian was able to use his influence to release a personal album. However, as discussed in previous chapters, the myth of rock and *Yaogun* was successfully established through the launch of an early music magazine, broadcasting, and intellectual interpretations of rock as the embodiment of the 'revolutionary, unconventional spirit' for a 'modern nation'. Meanwhile, under the influence of Cui Jian and the dual myths of rock and *Yaogun*, several other *Yaogun* bands emerged and became active through privately organised parties and performances, mainly in Beijing. These bands formed a relatively tight circle, supported by key members with resources (instruments, rehearsal space), driven by passion rather than commercialisation, and performing mainly for friends and an emerging audience of *Yaogun* enthusiasts. Notable bands from this era included Tang Dynasty (唐朝), Panthers (黑豹), Breathe (呼吸), ADO, and Cobra (眼镜蛇), with Cobra being the only band with female members (Capdeville-Zeng, 2001).

In 1990, Cui Jian and the band ADO initiated the 'Rock 'n' Roll on the New Long March' tour in several major cities in China. Meanwhile, a concert called 'The 1990 Modern Music Concert' (90 现代音乐会) was held at the Capital Stadium in Beijing. This concert was the first collective concert of *Yaogun* for the general public in China, in which all the above-mentioned *Yaogun* bands took part. After this concert, Tang Dynasty signed a contract with a record company called Magic Stone (魔岩), a subsidiary of the Rock Records Co. Ltd (滚石唱片) from Taiwan founded in 1991 by Zhang Peiren 张培仁 in Beijing. Two years later, Tang Dynasty released their heavy metal style debut album entitled *A Dream Return to Tang Dynasty* (梦回唐朝) with two official music videos produced by the Magic Stone, which established the band's important position in China's rock music scene. Later that year, Magic Stone released the overseas version of the album in Taiwan, Hong Kong, Japan, South Korea, and Southeast Asia. The album and music videos made a huge impact through Magic Stone's marketing and television broadcasts, not only in mainland China but also in East and Southeast Asia, and have become one of *Yaogun*'s classics to this day.

In 1994, two years after the release of *A Dream Return to Tang Dynasty*, my family replaced our old black and white television with a new SONY colour television, a famous Japanese brand and a luxury item for us at the time. I vividly remember watching Tang Dynasty's music video for 'A Dream Return to Tang Dynasty' on television in the mid-1990s and being immediately blown away by the combination of the speedy electronic guitar and the high-pitched scream of the vocals. In the middle of the song, the lead singer Ding Wu 丁武 recited excerpts from classic Chinese poetry in a rhetorically elevated, dramatic tone:[12]

忆昔开元全盛日
天下朋友皆胶漆
眼界无穷世界宽
安得广厦千万间！

> Remembering the days of Kaiyuan's (the prosperous era of the Tang Dynasty) full splendour
> When friends across the land were as adhesive as lacquer
> The boundless world before our eyes was vast
> How I wish for a million grand houses (to shelter all friends in need)

The lines Ding Wu recited were adapted from the poetry of Du Fu 杜甫, one of the greatest poets in Chinese literary history, renowned for his work during the Tang Dynasty. Every Chinese student knows Du Fu's name and studies his poems in school. Our literature textbooks taught us that Du Fu's works provide a deep and personal account of the social and political upheavals of his time. However, I had never imagined that Du Fu's poetry could be associated with heavy metal music. Suddenly, those lines came alive, recited to a loud music soundtrack, with images of four tall Chinese men in leather pants and long hair, standing in the vast, windy desert of western China with some ancient Buddhist temples in the background. It was an incredible sight on our brand-new television! As a Chinese teenager, for me the scene was both unfamiliar and exhilarating, with a strange sense of familiar intimacy. The Tang Dynasty represents a pinnacle of Chinese civilisation, prominently featured in all Chinese history textbooks and serving as a lasting source of national pride for the Chinese people, symbolising a prosperous and glorious past. Now this was portrayed on television through images of several Chinese men with massive, long hair, playing electric guitars and almost screaming in high-pitched voices – an image I'd only seen in music magazines featuring performers with foreign faces, and one that embodied the 'wild and free-spirited' Westerner. But at that time, there were four Chinese men reciting the classic Chinese poem I'd learnt by heart since primary school, in a wild, free-spirited, dramatic new way – it was all very strange, very new and very exciting.

In the mid-1990s, when I was about to enter junior high school, I had just heard of the term rock 'n' roll or *Yaogun*, vaguely associated with the name of Cui Jian; apart from the Tang Dynasty music video shown on television, I had no knowledge or listening experience of rock music, and I had no idea that I was living in an era marked by the emergence of *Yaogun* and the brief period of 'Chinese rock glory' that followed. This fleeting period in the history of *Yaogun* and modern China witnessed the harmonious yet temporary integration of the creativity of Chinese musicians and the idealism of 'rejuvenating Chinese culture' inherited from the 1980s, backed by capital from Taiwan and Hong Kong. In the following years, Magic Stone, under the leadership of its founder and key figures Zhang Peiren and Jia Minshu, with the support of Rock Records Ltd from Taiwan, and two other record companies backed by members and capital from Hong Kong, signed several *Yaogun* musicians and bands from mainland China, releasing a series of albums that profoundly influenced the history of Chinese rock music and captivated a generation of young Chinese audiences, including myself.

'China Fire': The Chinese alternative voices on the market

In the early 1990s, in addition to Magic Stone (魔岩), Red Star Records (红星音乐) was founded by Leslie Chan Kin Tim 陈健

添 and Earth Records (大地唱片) by Gene Lau 刘卓辉 in Beijing. Leslie Chan, who had worked for Warner Music Hong Kong Ltd, set up his own music management company and worked with local Hong Kong musicians before founding Red Star Records. Gene Lau, a Cantopop lyricist, had also been actively working with Hong Kong musicians for years before setting up Earth Records. Earth Records produced many popular albums with lasting impact in the 1990s and early 2000s, including the influential 1994 *Folksongs on Campus* (校园民谣), a compilation of several student songwriters/singers from major universities across China, which was the first album of this genre in mainland China. Also, Earth Records launched a wave of folk songs after the release of this album. The campus folk songs selected in the albums with various music videos produced by Earth Records quickly reached a majority of Chinese youth through radio and television programmes. These songs inspired many university students in the 1990s to compose their own songs or enter the local singing competitions in the hope of entering the emerging Chinese popular music landscape – including my younger uncle, who ignited my passion for popular music.

In the early 1990s, after a decade of opening and reform and the tragic shutdown of the 1989 student protests, these Hong Kong and Taiwan capital-backed record companies undoubtedly had economic ambitions in the vast mainland Chinese market, which was still a 'blank page'. However, the founders of these companies were also influenced by the heroic and poetic idealism of the 1980s mainland as well as by the dual myths of rock and *Yaogun*. Zhang Peiren, the founder of Magic Stone, confessed in interviews that he was fascinated when he first discovered the performance of Chinese rock bands such as Tang Dynasty in Beijing, and by founding the Magic Stone record label, he not only wanted to make money from *Yaogun* but also wanted to promote a 'special Chinese culture', comparable to the 'Chinese Renaissance' (中国文艺的复兴). He also sought to establish a 'Chinese new music' industry to resist the hegemony of the global music world, which was dominated by several international music/cultural corporations (Guo, 2007). Similarly, Gene Lau, the founder of Earth Record, had participated in demonstrations in support of Chinese students before the Tiananmen Square protests in Hong Kong. He wrote politically charged songs that remain important in Hong Kong's annual commemorations of the 1989 protests and other political movements.[13]

These companies released outstanding albums and compilations during the 1990s that had a significant impact on Chinese society, covering various styles and authentic moods of Chinese youth at the time. Red Star Records released *Red Star No. 1–3* (红星 1–3 号), a series of compilation albums featuring some of the most famous alternative/*Yaogun* singers of the 1990s; Earth Records released the *Folksongs on Campus* series and signed several female singer-composers, adding female figures to the mainly male-dominated alternative music scene. Among the vague 'Chinese modern music', the series called 'China Fire' (中国火) and three studio albums under the label 'The Three Prodigies' (魔岩三杰) produced by Magic Stone had a particularly important impact on the history of *Yaogun*.

Between 1991 and 1998, Magic Stone released the *China Fire I-III* (中国火 I-III) series, which focused on the *Yaogun* style, and three personal studio albums with a mix of *Yaogun*, folk, and punk styles under the label of 'The Three Prodigies': He Yong 何勇 – *The Garbage Dump* (垃圾场), Dou Wei 窦唯 – *Black Dreams* (黑梦), and Zhang Chu 张楚 – *Shameful Being Left Alone* (孤独的人是可耻的). In a China before the internet, albums released with elaborate marketing strategies and media coverage quickly reached the public. Although not every Chinese youth in the 1990s was into *Yaogun* or alternative music, almost everyone had heard of Tang Dynasty and 'The Three Prodigies' of Magic Stone. Many of my friends were introduced to *Yaogun* through these albums, and to this day I can still remember the lyrics to most of the songs on the albums I've listened to hundreds of times.

The legacy and influence of the 'China Fire' series and other *Yaogun*-style albums, represented by Tang Dynasty and 'The Three Prodigies' albums produced by Magic Stone, are significant and long-lasting. The heavy metal style combined with elements of Chinese classical culture from the Tang Dynasty has influenced the metal scene in China to this day. The poetic, realistic, and sometimes sarcastic lyrics of singer-songwriters such as Zhang Chu (*Shameful Being Left Alone*) and He Yong (*The Garbage Dump*) greatly influenced the development of independent singer-songwriters in China in the following years; they also stimulated and awakened the subtle personal emotions, often veiled and constrained by the collective mindset and strict social norms of Chinese society in a group of Chinese youth, including my 14-year-old self. The combined influence of these albums was encapsulated in the concept of '*Yaogun* Spirit' (摇滚精神), a motto in *Yaogun* circles and a legacy of the myths of rock and *Yaogun* represented by Cui

Jian. They embodied the ideals of individual freedom, anti-authoritarianism and dogmatism, poetic romanticism, as well as the thirst for knowledge and ideals of the 'enlightened liberal world' represented by the West, which are still cherished by many Chinese intellectuals and rock fans of the 'post-70s' and 'post-80s' generations (The 'post-70s' and 'post-80s' generations in China refer to people born in the 1970s and 1980s respectively. These cohorts represent distinct social groups shaped by China's rapid economic, cultural, and political changes after the opening up and reform policy.)

In parallel with the rise of Taiwanese and Hong Kong-backed record companies promoting *Yaogun* and alternative styles, an influx of popular music and idol culture from Hong Kong, Taiwan, and Western countries also entered the Chinese market. Since the mid-1990s, as material prosperity became more attainable, the Chinese public developed a growing appetite for fun and entertainment. With an expanding range of leisure activities and a new class of people enjoying greater financial comfort, relaxation and 'having a good time' became a natural priority.

As a result, enthusiasm for musical styles such as *Yaogun* and alternative rock – once associated with the idealism of the 1980s and collective concerns about freedom and social issues – began to wane. The shift in cultural priorities marked a turning point in the music industry. Despite these changes, labels such as Magic Stone, Red Star Records, and Earth Records remained key players in China's popular music market in the early 1990s. The albums they produced left a lasting legacy in the history of *Yaogun* and folk music and laid significant foundations for China's modern popular music industry.

In short, before the advent of the internet, these record labels played a crucial role in shaping the musical landscape. Their commercial and ideological commitment to *Yaogun* and independent songwriters deeply influenced the imagination, aesthetic sensibilities, and aspirations of many Chinese youth.

'Rock China: The Power of Music' live in Hong Kong: Ephemeral splendour

The sound and image of *Yaogun* produced by Magic Stone not only made a significant impact in mainland China but also influenced audiences in Hong Kong, Taiwan, and Malaysia through albums and concerts. On 17 December 1994, the most significant live show in *Yaogun* history, 'Rock China: the Power of Music' (摇滚中国乐势力), was held at the Hong Kong Coliseum (香港红磡体育馆). This event brought together Tang Dynasty and 'The Three Prodigies' – He Yong, Zhang Chu, and Dou Wei – at this iconic venue. Since its opening in 1983, the Coliseum has been a premier stage for high-profile concerts, significantly shaping Hong Kong's vibrant music scene and fostering cultural exchange within the industry. On the night of the concert, the Coliseum was packed with nearly 10,000 attendees and media from around the world.

'Rock China: The Power of Music' was curated by Zhang Peiren and produced by Magic Stone in collaboration with media and professionals from mainland China and Hong Kong. It was broadcast on Hong Kong television with a documentary directed by Qiu Litao 邱礼涛, marking a historic moment for Chinese rock music. For many Hong Kong audiences, it was their first taste of the vibrant rock scene in mainland China, and they were blown away!

The concert was a huge success. The three-and-a-half-hour event was marked by disbelief and excitement. The strict security rules of the Hong Kong Coliseum couldn't contain the tens of thousands of attendees who danced, screamed, stomped, and jumped throughout the show – an unusual sight for a typically reserved East Asian audience. Even the security personnel were swept up in the frenzy. After the concert, many seats were damaged by the overexcited audience, like the aftermath of Cui Jian's concert tours in the 1980s.

The next day, Hong Kong newspapers devoted extensive coverage to the concert, with headlines like 'Rock and roll souls, shocking Hong Kong', 'China rock, hitting Hong Kong', and '*Yaogun*, Very Chinese'. Numerous articles and cultural figures praised the enthusiastic response while pondering, 'What the hell is going on?' The concert left a lasting impression on the Hong Kong audience and had a ripple effect on *Yaogun*'s audience in mainland China through legal or pirated concert tapes and VCDs that later circulated in the mainland market. As the documentary only captured about 90 minutes of the concerts, Chinese rock fans have eagerly shared bootleg recordings of this concert on various video websites over the years.

At the end of the documentary, titled after the concert *Rock China: The Power of Music* (摇滚中国乐势力), a letter written by curator Zhang Peiren was featured. Today, it still resonates with the idealism and enthusiasm of the time:[14]

> I have long felt that this is an era of cultural inversion, where celebrities and idols are produced in packaging factories and popularised by the media, and people try to feed on the superficiality of entertainment while

ignoring the power of the real thing. The cultural phenomenon from the islands is hitting all Chinese places at a very fast pace, shallowness is replacing profundity, simplicity is replacing abundance, falsehood is replacing truth, and if this is the law of the business system, we may find that the cultural heritage left behind by the bubble economy is nothing more than a mass of bubbles after it has collapsed.

For the first time, they proved that idols are not static myths; in Hong Kong, the centre of China's entertainment industry, tens of thousands of people went crazy for the power of the 'real'. They showed that cultural nourishment from the rich mother earth could give rise to new horizons and imaginations. They saw the essence of music, a line connecting with the soul, prompting them to abandon their usual reserve and embrace the madness. This also influenced the record industry and media in Hong Kong and Taiwan, instilling the belief that business should only be a process, not the form of music.

Beyond the influence of the dual myths of rock and *Yaogun*, with their emphasis on 'being real' and anti-commercialism, reading Zhang Peiren's comments on the Hong Kong concert was particularly enlightening for me after nearly 20 years living abroad in France and the United Kingdom. I see Zhang's reflections as illustrating the enduring search for identity of someone who navigates between very different social, cultural, and political contexts; this was certainly related to Zhang's personal experiences and background, but it also reflected the wider social and historical influences on his perception of 'Chinese identity'. Chang Pei-ren was born and raised in Taiwan. Before founding

Magic Stone in Beijing, he worked in the Taiwanese music industry for many years, and hence was able to offer a different perspective as someone born and raised in mainland China under the CCP regime before the major economic reforms of the 1990s. To me, his letter reveals a clear personal desire for 'Chinese cultural rejuvenation' and a longing for a unified Chinese cultural identity at the beginning of the 'opening-up and reform' era, after a long period of geographical and ideological separation between Taiwan and mainland China, following the Japanese colonial occupation and the Chinese Civil War, which was similar to the 'Cold War' in Germany.

> For the first time, this show brings together people from China, Hong Kong, and Taiwan, all of whom have a strong mission and imagination for Chinese culture, and most of whom believe that the Chinese will have a more prosperous cultural landscape, and that it should not come from a fictional entertainment illusion, but from a more real and expansive creative force, and they all saw that hope in this concert.
>
> We have seen how each of them has invested their entire lives in their music over the past ten years, I have seen that every note is an extension of their lives, I have seen their deep affection for their music, and that the impact of the boom in Hong Kong is not the purpose of their creations, and that they have openly told the media in Hong Kong that Beijing is the source of their lives, and that China is the root of their creations. For all the people who want to get rich in the commercial system, their idea is almost incomprehensible, but we feel that this is the essence of Chinese new music, standing

on this foundation, we have more future to face, there are more distant tasks waiting, the success of the Hong Kong concert is just the beginning.

Taiwan's history is complex, shaped by a series of conflicts and occupations involving various parties. Its modern political landscape has been deeply influenced by the ideological struggle between the Chinese Communist Party (CCP) and the Chinese Nationalist Party (KMT). After the Chinese Civil War ended in 1949, the CCP established the People's Republic of China (PRC) on the mainland, while the KMT retreated to Taiwan and maintained the Republic of China (ROC).

By the 1990s, mainland China was undergoing significant economic reforms and rapid urbanisation after decades of political turmoil and economic stagnation. However, its music industry remained in its infancy. By contrast, Taiwan had lifted martial law in 1987 and embarked on democratic reforms that granted greater civil liberties, including freedom of speech and of the press. This more open and dynamic society fostered a thriving music industry that embraced global influences. With international companies integrating into Taiwan's cultural landscape, the music scene became vibrant yet increasingly market-driven, diverging sharply from the idealism that had defined *Yaogun* and rock music in mainland China during the 1980s.

Against this backdrop, Zhang Peiren's desire for an authentic 'new Chinese culture' – one untainted by 'soulless' commercialism and profit-driven motives – feels like a natural reaction to the evolving music industry.

Unfortunately, Zhang's vision of the success of the Hong Kong concert as the beginning of a glorious era for Chinese rock did not materialise. After that concert, the *Yaogun* scene stagnated for several years, and the dream of 'rejuvenating Chinese culture', which culminated in the 'Rock China' concert in Hong Kong, turned out to be an illusory and idealistic bubble, a fleeting glory, and no one ever knows what 'more distant tasks await' as Zhang claimed in his letter, after he closed the Magic Stone and left mainland China in the late 1990s. However, although the idealism and romance of *Yaogun* and rock were fleeting, and Magic Stone, Red Star, and Earth Records gradually closed in the early 2000s, their impact on the Chinese music landscape remains profound.

Facing the 'reality': Modern Sky, market logic, and the dissolution of myths

After the collective youthful idealism of the 1980s – marked by a quest for personal freedom and social change – a new generation of musicians emerged in the 1990s with different experiences, values, and aspirations. Born into the era of economic reform and opening up, they had witnessed both economic hardship and the rapid transformation of Chinese society. Unlike their predecessors, they grew up in a relatively freer social environment, with greater individual autonomy and a wider range of cultural and entertainment influences.

Their music reflected not only personal emotions but also critical observations of society and its contradictions. As a result, the Chinese rock scene of the late 1990s became increasingly diverse, encompassing genres such as heavy metal, punk, folk, and electronic music. This stylistic expansion reflected the complexity of a rapidly changing China.

In this context, *Yaogun* found itself at a crossroads. While it had built a solid foundation and loyal fan base through the production and marketing of the early record companies backed by Hong Kong and Taiwan, it also faced challenges and uncertainties in the rapidly changing Chinese society and music industry. As *Yaogun* continued to evolve, it navigated the challenge of preserving its core values and spirit – rooted in the dual myths – while adapting to the new realities of the music market and shifting audience preferences. The need to strike this balance became a central concern, as the genre grappled with the opportunities and threats posed by technological advancements, industrialisation, and the increasing commercialisation of popular music in China.

In the summer of 1998, I graduated from junior high school with high honours and was promoted to one of the best high schools in Kunming. As a reward, my father bought me a computer: a bulky Lenovo computer. At that time, personal computers had just been launched in China, and they cost more than 9,000 RMB, which was equivalent to my parents' annual income. It was also the first computer I ever used with Windows 98, and it opened another window to a new world of technology and gadgetry.

Meanwhile, about a year after discovering *Yaogun* and the alternative voices to which I could relate my subtle feelings, I became more acquainted with the music genre called rock 'n' roll through pirated cassettes and videotapes, magazines, a few radio programmes, and some music videos broadcast on television. In the process, I also became more familiar with the styles and spirit of the *Yaogun* singers in the early 1990s. Inspired by the music and lyrics of these singers, I began to look at the lives of the people around me in a slightly different way, and began to notice the impacts of rapid social transformation on people's personal lives, as well as the injustices, frustrations, and doubts in the society that I had rarely seen before as a carefree junior high-school girl with good grades.

One of the most striking moments in my early encounters with rock music was watching a pirated video compact disc (VCD) of a live performance of Pink Floyd's *Another Brick in the Wall (Part 2)*. I played it on my newly purchased personal computer – and the experience was unforgettable.

I can still vividly recall the shock and awe I felt when I saw the now-iconic theatrical scene in which children join the band on stage – not just to jump and chant but also to interact with a giant, grotesque grinding machine as part of the performance's dark and symbolic narrative. Until that moment, I had always regarded education and teachers in a purely positive light. Growing up under the influence of Confucian ideals, I had been taught that a person could achieve excellence only through diligent study and the guidance of good teachers. Although I sometimes complained about the increasingly heavy workload and the pressure to maintain top grades, I had never questioned the system itself.

But watching that particular scene of *Another Brick in the Wall* forced me to confront a radically different perspective – one that challenged the very foundation of what I had always taken for granted. The imagery was unsettling: children marching in uniform, stripped of individuality, forced into conformity until they became faceless products of an unyielding system. The grinding machine metaphor was particularly disturbing and scary – suggesting that education, rather than being a path to enlightenment, could also be a mechanism of control that crushes an individual. The line 'We don't need no education' felt particularly subversive when it came from a group of young students who were about my age at the time.

This realisation planted a seed of critical thinking in me. Up to that point, I had largely benefited from the education system – I had just been awarded a luxury personal computer for my good grades! In China, academic success was equated with future prosperity. The measure of a 'good student' in Chinese society was (and still is) simple: good grades led to prestigious universities, which led to a good job, a good job guaranteed a good future/good life, and a good life, by social consensus, meant a lifestyle of wealth or a respected title. But this moment of epiphany made me think about how education could also function as an instrument of social conformity – rewarding obedience while suppressing individuality.

Pink Floyd's performance didn't just challenge my views on education; it made me start thinking more deeply about the structures that shape people's lives. It was one of my first personal experiences of music as a tool of critique, a medium that could challenge authority and expose uncomfortable realities that were rarely broadcast in mainstream Chinese media. This realisation stayed with me – not only shaping my approach to *Yaogun* and music in general but also deepening my appreciation of art as a whole. It also initiated my lifelong interest in exploring the relationship between artistic expression, personal perception, and the complexities of society – a quest that would continue to inform my intellectual and spiritual pursuits in the years to come.

The early albums produced by Magic Stone also had a great impact on me. I can still vividly recall some of the lyrics and melodies from the 'China Fire' series and the albums by 'The Three Prodigies':[15]

> The world we live in is a garbage dump, people are like worms
> > They fight with each other, they eat heartily and they shit out thoughts.
> > The world we live in is like a garbage dump
> > You have no choice but to live on illusions
> > Some diet, others starve
> > Is there hope? Is there any hope? Is there any hope?
> > > ('Garbage Dump' 《垃圾场》- He Yong 何勇)

> Miss Zhao's surname is Zhao, the Zhao of Zhao, Qian, Sun and Li
> You'll know her name without guessing
> You can call her Zhao Li, Little Zhao Or Zhao Lili
> She still lives with her parents
> There she can eat and rest
> She's got a boyfriend and can go pamper herself to a man.

> She has a job that won't last long
> It's not much money and she won't stay until she retires
> There's only one situation that makes her sad
> When someone else's dress is better than hers
>
> ('Miss Zhao' 《赵小姐》 - Zhang Chu 张楚)

'Garbage Dump' resonated deeply with me, partly because of He Yong's screaming voice and the raw energy of anger conveyed by his performance. The lyrics captured the stark contrasts and widening gaps between social classes in the 1990s, painting a bleak picture of a world divided by material inequality, where the pursuit of wealth overshadowed the idealism that had once been central to cultural discourse – a bleak picture that was hard to see through my own eyes: a 15-year-old, good student with an optimistic expectation for the future at the time. From today's perspective, it reflected a society moving away from collective idealistic dreams towards hedonism and consumerism – what Zhang Peiren, the founder of Magic Stone, described as an existence 'devoid of soul'.

Meanwhile, 'Miss Zhao' struck me in a different way. Zhang Chu's quiet, lazy voice and piercing lyrics revealed the gradual erasure of individuality and the increasing conformity that had begun to define mainstream society in the late 1990s. The character of Miss Zhao, an ordinary Chinese young woman content with routine and superficial desires, epitomised the numbness and apathy that had begun to permeate urban life. Both songs opened my eyes to the contradictions and complexities of rapidly changing Chinese society.

Around 1998, amid the soundscape of *Yaogun* represented by Cui Jian, Tang Dynasty, and 'The Three Prodigies', a brand-new Chinese band appeared on television with a music video for the song of the same name from their first album, 'Great!?' (《好极了！？》). The band's name was Sober (清醒), and they were the first Chinese band to feature a self-assigned English name on their album cover and on MTV. Sober was composed of four young, slim Chinese men with short, conventional haircuts, dressed in neat shirts, fitting trousers, and suits. The lead singer sported a tailored wool coat – a very trendy and English-inspired look. This was totally different from the previous rock and *Yaogun* bands or musicians I knew. The music (melodies and rhythms) as well as visual elements in Sober's MTV video resembled those of the Beatles. Their most popular song, 'Great!?', featured only four or five lines of lyrics, describing the repetitive, mundane experience of an ordinary office worker:

> It's been a busy, busy day.
> I'm working.
> I can't stop.
> Who did I give Monday and Tuesday to?
> Who did I give Wednesday and Thursday?
> Who did I give Friday and Saturday?
> Who do I give Sunday to?
> All right, all right, all right, all right!
>
> ('Great!?' 《好极了！？》 - Sober 清醒))

In the late 1990s, China's state-owned enterprises (SOEs) faced profound challenges as economic reforms intensified. Once the backbone of the nation's planned economy, SOEs had become overstaffed, indebted, and burdened by outdated management practices. The heavy subsidies they received strained government finances and stifled broader economic growth. Meanwhile, the rise of private and foreign-invested enterprises underscored the urgent need for SOEs to either adapt or face obsolescence. In response, Premier Zhu Rongji 朱镕基, who served from 1998 to 2003, spearheaded a sweeping reform initiative that played a pivotal role in steering China towards a more market-oriented system.

This period marked a critical transition in China's economic history, but the reforms came at a significant social cost. Mass layoffs and restructuring led to widespread unemployment, exacerbating social inequality and instability. The dismantling of the 'Iron Rice Bowl' （铁饭碗） – a term symbolising the guaranteed lifetime employment and benefits provided by the SOEs – represented a profound shift in the social contract between the state and its citizens. The lives of millions of workers who had relied on state employment for security were suddenly plunged into uncertainty, reflecting the painful realities of this economic transition.

Despite these social challenges, the reforms were crucial in modernising China's economy. They also allowed foreign companies to compete on a more level playing field, leading to a surge in foreign direct investment as multinationals sought to capitalise on China's burgeoning market. These changes laid the foundation for the rapid economic growth that followed, highlighting both the complexity and necessity of transitioning from a planned economy to a market-driven one.

Amid these sweeping changes, a new urban middle class began to emerge in China. Composed of young professionals working in the private sector or for international companies, this 'white-collar' workforce enjoyed greater social status and financial security. They began to develop their own lifestyle – characterised by fashion, consumer choices, and cultural tastes – that was heavily influenced by Western media, particularly from the United States. The 'American dream' became a powerful symbol for this newly formed Chinese middle class, shaping their aspirations and defining their place in the evolving social landscape.

It was at this crucial juncture in China's socio-economic history that I first encountered Sober, a band whose music and style resonated deeply with the changing cultural landscape. The fashion symbols and sense of ennui expressed in their song 'Great?!' captured a new subjectivity and emotional landscape that was unfamiliar to me at the time. As a junior high school graduate, I was impressed by the band's cosmopolitan image, their seamless blend of Chinese and English, and the modern aesthetic of their record label, Modern Sky. This was a stark departure from the cultural norms I had known, and it felt refreshingly new.

Reflecting on the lyrics and music video of 'Great?!' today, I can clearly see how they encapsulated the emotions of the emerging urban middle class – boredom and restlessness – feelings unfamiliar to many former SOE employees still grappling with the uncertainties of the new economy. But for me, Sober's music symbolised the arrival of something entirely new – a cultural shift that reflected the wider economic and social changes taking place in China in the late 1990s.

The founding of Modern Sky Records (摩登天空) in 1997 signalled a decisive turning point for *Yaogun*. By promoting and embracing a distinctly more 'cosmopolitan' and fashionable, as well as more entertaining, image of Chinese rock and alternative music, it represented a fundamental shift in Chinese society and the urban music landscape; the lifestyles represented by the music and albums under the labels of Modern Sky were illustrations of the emerging Chinese youth culture after a decade of market-economy transformation in the 1990s in China. They also marked the new subjectivities of Chinese urban youth. In a sense, Modern Sky symbolically heralded the dismantling of the structure and logic of the dual myths of 'revolutionary' rock and *Yaogun* that had been established in the 1990s. Meanwhile, it also marked a radical shift in the relationship between the '*Yaogun* circles' (摇滚圈子) formed in the 1990s and the rockers who formed them. These circles were deeply bound to a certain hierarchical structure, centralised in Beijing, and male-dominated (Capdeville-Zeng, 2001).

Modern Sky Records was established in Beijing in December 1997 by Shen Lihui 沈黎辉, the lead singer of the Beijing-based alternative band Sober. By 2002, the company had evolved into Modern Sky Entertainment Co., Ltd, rapidly becoming a major driving force in China's alternative music scene and youth culture. The company expanded its operations, launching its own music magazine, venturing into video production and graphic design, and founding the Strawberry Music Festival in 2009. By 2014, Modern Sky had solidified its role as a key player in the Chinese music industry, demonstrating a keen understanding of the trajectory of 'new Chinese music' in an increasingly globalised world.

As discussed in Chapter 3, Chinese modernity has often been intertwined with the coloniality or cultural imperialism of

Euro-US centric thought – a intertwining dynamic that, whether consciously or not, has shaped China's cultural trajectory in the twentieth century. The rise of Modern Sky in the late 1990s echoed the social ambitions of 1920s Shanghai, where there was a strong desire to modernise China along Western lines. During the 1990s, popular music from Hong Kong, Taiwan, Europe, and the United States became increasingly accessible in mainland China. As a result, new bands began forming and were given opportunities to perform not only at underground parties but also in newly emerging venues across the country. Shen Lihui himself acknowledged that Modern Sky was a mirror of China's socio-cultural environment in the late 1990s. The company symbolised a shift towards a more pragmatic, materialistic, and entertainment-oriented society within a globalised context.

Researcher Jonathan Campbell aptly noted that the *Yaogun* scene expanded – both geographically and stylistically – as more musicians joined the ranks of rock: 'Meanwhile, as the nation grew more accustomed to its new, if ever shifting, identity as a member of the rest of the world, *Yaogun* started to look less like an enemy and more like just one of those things with which a modern inhabitant of the globe might, if they wanted, deal' (2011: 141).

Shen Lihui founded Modern Sky at a time when the Chinese music industry was in need of a standardised business structure. His initial motivation was straightforward: to produce his own band's album and to establish a new business model for the Chinese music industry. In fact, Modern Sky not only redefined the structure of the popular music business in China but also introduced a new ideology. *Yaogun*, once viewed as a revolutionary and non-commercial genre epitomised by artists such as Cui Jian and Tang Dynasty, or portrayed by early record labels like Magic Stone – which claimed to represent the spirit of the times, society, and an entire generation – was reimagined as popular music for the masses. In other words, once considered revolutionary, *Yaogun* was now seen less as a threat and more as just another aspect of modern life in China (Lu, 2021). This aligns with Campbell's observation that *Yaogun* had become just another facet of global modernity.

Ultimately, Modern Sky sought to deconstruct the myth of both rock and *Yaogun*. The new generation of Chinese musicians, represented by Shen Lihui, bore a lighter ideological burden compared to their predecessors. In essence, the founding of Modern Sky marked a turning point in China's cultural landscape, reflecting a broader societal shift towards market logic and the dissolution of the revolutionary myths that had once defined *Yaogun*. Shen's vision of creating a new music business model has been realised through Modern Sky's two decades of development, with evolving ambitions along the way. By 2021, Modern Sky Entertainment Co., Ltd had transformed into a lifestyle company centred on the concept of 'Music+', focusing on the exploration of youth aesthetics and lifestyle, with a global reach. Since 2017, Modern Sky UK has established itself as a label in Liverpool, becoming a part of the global Modern Sky Entertainment family with offices in Beijing, Berlin, New York, and London. The home page of Modern Sky UK's official website declares: 'Influence youth culture globally', reflecting the company's ambition to become a global entertainment entity.

5 'New Sound of Beijing' and '*Dakou* generation': 'New clothes, new life!'

New Sound of Beijing Movement: 'This is Our Time!'

> The day has finally come,
>
> When everything has changed.
>
> There is no more worry, everything is love.
>
> la la la la la la la la la la la la
>
> This is our time!
>
> la la la la la la la la
>
> This is our time![16]
>
> – 'This Is Our Time!'《这是我们的时代》(New Pants 新裤子)

The phrase 'New Sound of Beijing' (北京新声) first appeared in the promotional material for the debut album of Sober, a band fronted by Shen Lihui, who also founded Modern Sky Records. The phrase gained further prominence with the release of Modern Sky Records' first compilation album, *Modern Sky I* (摩登天空 I), which featured many emerging bands and alternative musicians in the 1990s known outside the 'old *Yaogun* circle', including Sober and 'China's first real electronic band' Supermarket (超级市场). In 1999, renowned *Yaogun* critic Yan Jun 颜峻 and cultural activist Ou Ning 欧宁 solidified the concept with the publication of a book titled *The New Sound of Beijing* (北京新声). This title encapsulated a pivotal moment in Chinese popular music and symbolised a shift in the cultural landscape of the late 1990s (Nie *et al.*, 1999).

Meanwhile, from 1994 to 1998, a wave of new bands entered Beijing's music scene, though many of these musicians came from regions outside the capital and gathered in the outskirts of Beijing city, living in humble surroundings, with simple equipment and no stable source of income, rehearsing on their own, fighting for gigs, and hoping to one day become part of the mainstream rock market. Throughout the 1990s, they gradually formed an underground community of Chinese alternative music, along with other artists with similar backgrounds.

Published in 1999, *New Sound of Beijing* chronicled the rise of ten Chinese 'independent' bands, using a mix of text, images, interviews, and songs to vividly portray a burgeoning musical movement. Many of the members of these bands had some experience living in the underground community in the suburbs of Beijing. The bands included Catcher in the Rye (麦田守望者),

Underground Baby (地下婴儿), Zi Yue (子曰), No. 43 Baojiajie Road (鲍家街 43 号), Zhang Qianqian (张浅潜), Supermarket (超级市场), Autumn Bugs (秋天的虫子), New Pants (新裤子), Flowers (花儿), and Sober (清醒). In the book's introduction, chief editor Ou Ning noted that the 'New Sound of Beijing' had become synonymous with a wave of creativity and independence in the Chinese music scene and named it the 'New Sound of Beijing Movement'.

Reinterpreting individualism in music

A defining characteristic of the New Sound of Beijing Movement was its emphasis on individualism. While earlier generations of Chinese rockers also expressed personal voices, this new wave introduced a 'new individual story', aimed at a different audience. Andreas Steen (2000) observes that this movement focused on individual narratives, but with a fresh approach that deviated from traditional rock and *Yaogun* myths. Shen Lihui, both in interviews and in Sober's lyrics, also emphasised a straightforward philosophy: 'Tell your own stories, express your own feelings, and have fun in your own corner', consciously avoiding the sociopolitical themes traditionally linked to rock and *Yaogun* music (Steen, 2000).

The musicians featured in *New Sound of Beijing* were born between 1969 and 1983, experiencing their formative years in major Chinese cities during the 1980s and 1990s. Unlike their parents, for whom popular music often symbolised a moral conviction or an absolute ideal, this new generation viewed music as entertainment. Before the internet became widely accessible in China in the late 1990s, these musicians were influenced by the pirated and clandestine circulation of cassettes and CDs 'with a cut', known as *Dakou* cassettes and CDs, which brought Western music products into China as plastic waste. Together they embodied the archetype of the 'new cosmopolitan city dweller' (Ou, 1999:3).

Shifting focus: From ideological protest to personal expression

Cui Jian, often hailed as the godfather of Chinese rock, had already hinted at this shift in his 1998 song 'Quack' （混子）from the album *The Power of the Powerless* (无能的力量). In the song, Cui sings, 'The new era has arrived; the conflicts between all idealisms no longer exist' （新的时代到了, 理想间的斗争已经不复存在了）(Cui, 1998). His lyrics capture well the changing mindsets of the younger generation, who were beginning to move away from viewing the world through a lens of ideological conflict and instead turned inwards, focusing on personal, day-to-day experiences and feelings.

The introduction to the *New Sound of Beijing* collection emphasises the transformative power of music and the lifestyle changes represented by the ten groups featured. The authors write: 'Since its birth, new music has begun to change the history of conscience. The new world is already here. The suppressed beauty and the forgotten imagination are coming to us: a new life, new emotions, a new way of thinking, new clothes and new languages' (Ou, 1999:4). This passage encapsulates the New Sound of Beijing Movement as more than a musical movement; it was a broader cultural phenomenon that signalled a new era with new individual subjectivities in Chinese society.

Finally, Ou Ning's comment in the foreword to *New Sound of Beijing* accurately summed up the form and essence of the movement (Nie *et al.*, 1999):¹⁷

> The cultural phenomenon we call The New Sound of Beijing consists of two main categories of participants – musicians and music lovers, all born in the 1970s and 1980s, all grown up with records 'with a cut' (*Dakou* 打口), they have more sonic experiences than their parents, their interests are also much more varied. Music is just one part of their hobbies, not the only one, and certainly not their whole life. So they don't have idealistic and abstract illusions about music, and they always remain pragmatic.
> In terms of musical styles, they mix several elements, including pop-punk, experimental guitar folk music, noise music, experimental electronic music, etc. They don't limit themselves to a heart-rending reflection on how Chinese music can be heard on a global scale. Instead, they enter directly into the international musical context.
> In terms of musical content, they are based on the real experiences of everyday life and represent playfulness and a certain sensible hedonism.
> In terms of its origins, it is a product of China's sweeping social transformation in the 1990s.

Dakou: From unwanted plastic waste to spiritual nourishment in a different world

In the *New Sound of Beijing*, the authors claimed to have not only brought 'new music, new clothes, and new life' through some emerging bands, but also introduced and highlighted a concept known as the 'Dakou generation' (打口一代). The term originally referred to a cultural phenomenon in China from the mid-1990s to the early 2000s, in which illegal 'cut out' cassettes and CDs – the surplus of the Western music market imported as plastic waste – were 'recycled' and secretly circulated in the black market in China.[18] It also referred to the creation of the concept of the 'Dakou generation', or 'generation with a cut', a specific group of Chinese youth who were heavily influenced and shaped by the Dakou phenomenon during this period. This group shared common traits such as a non-systematic musical knowledge by self-education through the Dakou products, which was outside any cultural context or historical framework; an emphasis on 'authenticity' and 'non-conformist' lifestyles; a critical perspective on society and personal life; as well as a rejection of both orthodox political and social norms and market logic and cultural commodification. It was probably the last generation of Chinese youth to be clearly labelled after a specific cultural phenomenon – one that arose from a confluence of factors, including a reaction against the dogmatic and hierarchical social/cultural environment, the underground and subcultural narratives, and unique economic channels and drivers.

A personal anecdote: My first encounter with Dakou cassettes

Around the summer of 1998, in my hometown of Kunming city, China, I had just entered one of the best senior high schools in the city. School life was monotonous, filled with tightly scheduled classes, heavy homework load, motivational speeches from teachers and parents about the importance of senior high school, and the increasingly stressful study environment due to competition with peers. The final exam of the Chinese senior high school, the *gaokao*, was a fiercely competitive national entrance exam that determined whether students could enter top-ranked universities based on their grades. Graduating from top-ranked Chinese universities offers many young people greater opportunities to find 'top-ranked' jobs with high salaries and social status, making the *gaokao* one of the most important opportunities in life for many Chinese young people, especially those with fewer financial, social, and networking resources. This made it extremely important and stressful for both students and parents.

During my three years of senior high school, listening to rock or alternative music became the highlight of my otherwise monotonous days. Twice a week, I would tune in to a special local radio programme with a DJ who knew about rock and alternative music while doing my homework. Meanwhile, as a newcomer to the world of rock and *Yaogun* music – and before the internet became the main channel of information in everyday life in China – I eagerly searched for any information or audiovisual products related to rock or alternative music. I would scour music magazines or listen to radio programmes, seeking anything I could find. However, the record stores primarily stocked mainstream pop music from Hong Kong and Taiwan, along with a few 'Western classics or pop-folk music icons' such as The Carpenters, John Denver, and Simon & Garfunkel.

One afternoon, while walking along a road near Yunnan University (the city's main university), I saw a man sitting next to a stall off the road with some cassettes laid out. Intrigued, I walked over to take a closer look. All the cassettes featured foreign musicians or bands with English labels, and I didn't recognise any of them. Each cassette cost about ten yuan, like a normal pop cassette in a record store, but they all had a small 'cut' on the edge that I didn't understand.

The man noticed my interest but also that I hesitated to choose one. He approached me and, in a low voice, said, 'These are just a few samples. If you're interested, I have a lot more.'

'Really? Can I see them?' I replied eagerly.
'Sure, but they're not here. If you follow me, I can show you.'

As a 16-year-old high school student, following a random man to an unknown place seemed like a crazy and risky decision – especially in the 1990s, when theft and other social crimes were not uncommon in cities. But my passion and thirst for different music, combined with my great curiosity, made me say 'yes' without thinking too much. I followed him to a nearby old residential area and eventually entered a simple room, where he pulled out a large box filled with all kinds of 'foreign music' cassettes – all marked with a cut – from under the bed.

I don't remember if I ended up buying any cassettes that day, but I somehow left the room and the neighbourhood safe and sound. What I didn't realise at the time was that this was my first encounter with *Dakou* cassettes – a phenomenon that was unique to China during the specific period between late 1990s and mid-2000s. *Dakou* cassettes (and CDs later) helped millions of Chinese youth gain 'equal' access to a wide range of cultural products – music, film, and television – from the outside world, bypassing the state censorship and control, at affordable prices. This phenomenon became a source of self-education for a generation in China. It deeply influenced and shaped the artistic knowledge, lifestyles, and subjectivities of many people during that period, and it has ultimately changed the way an entire generation lived and thought when looking back from today.

The story of *Dakou*: A case study about consumerism and colonial modernity

The term *Dakou* (打口) literally means 'to make a cut' in Chinese. It refers to cassettes and CDs of original music that have been deliberately damaged – often with a cut along the edge or a punched hole – rendering some songs unlistenable. However, most of the tracks were left intact and, in the case of cassettes, could often be restored with simple repairs. These items were surplus audio products, originally manufactured by major record companies for the North American and European markets. Due to the high cost of destruction and the relatively lax trade regulations and need for raw materials in some South Asian countries, many of these products were not destroyed but exported to Asia at very low prices as actual plastic waste. These damaged cassettes and CDs were then shipped to China, sometimes via Japan or Hong Kong, and sold discreetly in record shops and on the black market in Chinese cities.

In the late 1990s, *Dakou* cassettes and CDs became a vital gateway for young Chinese music lovers to explore different musical genres from around the world – pop, folk, classical, jazz, blues, indie, and rock 'n' roll. On the one hand, the Chinese authorities maintained strict control over imported audiovisual products. On

Figure 5: Pictures of a *Dakou* CD from personal collection. A compilation of film music – a French edition I bought in Beijing in the early 2000s – which I took with me to France and then to the United Kingdom, and still listen to occasionally.

the other hand, the high cost of officially imported music products made it inaccessible to the average Chinese family, whose income was still quite limited in the 1990s. For many, me included, *Dakou* cassettes and CDs were often the only affordable means of discovering a wider range of global music, especially rock and alternative music, which at the time were considered marginal and 'rebellious'.

By the late 1990s and early 2000s, almost every Chinese rock music fan had bought or listened to some *Dakou* cassettes or CDs through underground channels in major cities. Many of these listeners would go on to form rock bands, create music magazines, or set up websites and online radio stations. In this way, the *Dakou* phenomenon significantly shaped the landscape of Chinese rock and alternative music long before the internet and music streaming platforms became dominant.

The *Dakou* phenomenon was the result of a unique confluence of factors that that came together at a particular time in China: the insatiable thirst for 'new' music and cultural resources among a group of Chinese youth in the 1990s; the rise of underground subcultures; and an economic anomaly rooted in the overproduction of music in the United States and Europe. Together, these forces fuelled a movement that left an indelible mark on China's music scene and a generation of Chinese youth.

The myth of Nirvana, Kurt Cobain, and the imagination of underground culture

In 1996, Hao Fang 郝舫, one of China's most influential rock critics and cultural figures, published a biographical book about Kurt Cobain, the lead singer of the alternative rock band Nirvana, entitled 灿烂涅槃：柯特柯本的一生 (*Nirvana Grandiose: The Life of Kurt Cobain*). This work, which was widely distributed in China and republished in 1998 and 2006, had a significant impact on Chinese rock fans and the '*Dakou* generation'. In the book, Hao Fang not only chronicled Kurt Cobain's musical achievements, but he also delved into the inner turmoil, isolation, and relentless pursuit of 'freedom' and self-expression that characterised the legendary lead singer of Nirvana. The book painted a complex portrait of Cobain, depicting both his ground-breaking contributions to music and the immense personal pain he endured under the pressures of fame.

A key moment in Hao Fang's narrative is his quotation of the phrase, 'It's better to burn out than to fade away', incorporated by Kurt Cobain into his 1994 suicide note and translated into Chinese by Hao Fang (与其苟延残喘，不如从容燃烧). The phrase was taken from the lyrics of Neil Young's song, 'Hey Hey, My My', but many Chinese readers took it to be Cobain's last words. The message and attitude conveyed by the phrase somehow resonated deeply with China's rock musicians and fans of the late 1990s and early 2000s (the 'Dakou generation'), becoming a motto and symbol of their identity and vision of life.

The 'Dakou generation', shaped by their access to damaged but playable Western music CDs through the guidance of music critics and self-education, saw Cobain as an underground hero. For many, Cobain's tragic end, along with these lyrics, encapsulated the idea of an alternative rock icon who rejected mainstream values, much like China's first rock hero Cui Jian, who also retreated from the public sphere under government censorship and restrictions on large-scale performances for many years after the 1980s. In China, where grunge was a new and electrifying wave, Cobain's face and famous motto became ubiquitous on posters at underground concerts in the early 2000s. Again, like the myth of rock constructed by music magazines and music critics in the early 1990s, the myth of the underground was constructed by Hao Fang's book and its portrayal of the life of Kurt Cobain. This time, however, Chinese rock fans could not only imagine the 'underground hero' through words and books, but they could also access his actual music, sound, and images via the clandestine Dakou CDs circulated all around China from the mid-1990s.

Cobain's suicide in 1994 became a defining moment, perfectly in keeping with the myth of the underground of the 1990s, embodied in the popular motto that echoed among young rock fans. Cobain's life – and death – cemented his status as an underground hero, another symbol of the anti-establishment icon, revered for rejecting the commodified image of the rock star and embracing a DIY ethic that appealed strongly to the Chinese underground scene. In the late 1990s, for example, the price of a Nirvana *Dakou* CD rose by around 80–100 yuan, about a quarter of the average monthly wage at the time, but many Chinese rock fans still bought it without hesitation.

Hao Fang attributes the profound influence of his book to the growing social discontent among Chinese urban youth in the late 1990s. Many teenagers, even those unfamiliar with rock music, found in Kurt Cobain a figure with whom they could identify. They connected fragments of Cobain's personal struggles to their own lives, often expressing their dissatisfaction with their families, schools, and society, which not only put great pressure on the younger generations to 'succeed', but also discouraged them from being 'different, original, and individualistic'. Hao Fang later received many letters from these young people expressing their anger at the pressures of their daily lives. For them, the book became an important mental weapon to resist an environment they felt was suffocating them (Campbell, 2011).

Jonathan Campbell (2011: 138), in his work on Chinese rock, quotes an extract from one such letter to Hao Fang: 'We inevitably identified with him (Kurt Cobain) because we shared the same anger, irony and introspection that he had, and these were common feelings at the time.' This sentiment underlines how Chinese youth in the 1990s found resonance in Cobain's defiance, using him as a vessel to express their own alienation and disillusionment.

The widespread embrace of Cobain as an underground rock icon in China was, as Hao Fang later acknowledged, a mixture of historical coincidence and 'inevitable misunderstanding' (必然的误解). Much like the myth surrounding Cui Jian in the 1980s, Chinese youth needed a figure to embody their rejection of mainstream values, including family expectations and social norms, and the idealised 'new Chinese youth model' that the state sought to promote. Cobain's image offered them a social space – whether real or imagined – where they could articulate their feelings of loss, frustration, and rebellion.

Hao Fang himself later reflected on the unintended impact of his work, noting that he never anticipated such a profound effect when he wrote the book. As he remarked in Campbell's book, 'When you write a book, you can never think about how it will influence people. You can't think about anything when you write – you can't think too much about yourself – but other people can take what you have written very seriously' (Campbell, 2011: 137). In the end, Cobain, through Hao Fang's pen, became not just a symbolic figure of American grunge rebel, but a transcendent symbol for a generation of Chinese youth searching for meaning in an increasingly globalised and yet still constricted society.

Dakou business: Accidental subversion and colonial modernity

The *Dakou* business is a mystery, eliciting more questions than answers. Who were the sellers of *Dakou* cassettes or CDs?

What drove their practices, and how did they operate? To this day, the sector remains underground and legally ambiguous. Like music piracy in China and other parts of the world, the *Dakou* trade resists easy categorisation and defies any 'official' or 'legitimate' narrative. However, by drawing on personal interviews and sources from secondary literature – such as a report dedicated to the *Dakou* business in one of China's most influential rock and underground music magazines, *So Rock!* (我爱摇滚乐Vol.11), and the podcast '*Dakou*: Mixtape' produced by Radiolab（Radiolab, 22 October 2021）– we can sketch a rough outline of this hidden industry. This section attempts to trace the roles and perspectives of *Dakou* sellers, or 'distribution agents', by illustrating their informal networks and practices from the story told by one former *Dakou* CD seller, Daodao (pseudonym), whose account sheds light on the mechanics of this unregulated trade. I have chosen to illustrate this invisible facet of history with the transcript of the stories told by Daodao. Daodao also founded one of China's first online 'alternative music' radios with its own forums for registered members, called The Crow Radio乌鸦电台 (2002.10–2010.10), which has had a significant impact on rock and alternative music fans belonging to the '*Dakou* generation' in the first decade of the twenty-first century, including myself.

The texts presented below are transcriptions of oral histories told by Daodao, a former *Dakou* CD seller. These accounts were translated from Chinese from several email exchanges I had with him. While the transcript has been trimmed for brevity, it remains a crucial piece in illustrating the hidden networks of the *Dakou* trade.[19]

My personal connection to the *Dakou* business extends beyond research – it shaped my own musical education and that of many of my peers during the late 1990s and early 2000s. The influx of *Dakou* products enabled an entire generation to self-educate through music, influencing not only listeners like me but also many future rock musicians, music industry founders, and cultural pioneers in China.

'The *Dakou* Years' (打口岁月), told by Daodao (pseudonym)

[Edited transcript]

Oddly enough, the emergence of *Dakou* cassettes in China was a by-product of the plastic waste trade. In the early 1990s, coastal cities such as Shantou (汕头) in Guangdong Province became centres of light manufacturing, requiring huge amounts of plastic. Rather than storing or destroying unsold tapes and CDs, Western record companies dumped them as actual waste, which was then exported by barge to Asian countries. In Guangdong, these shipments were dismantled in recycling factories, where workers sorted the materials.

At first, the discarded cassettes and CDs were discovered by music fans looking for scarce resources. Gradually, small entrepreneurs – often factory workers – began to collect and sell them. These 'small bosses' memorised album covers and set aside sought-after items before they were processed as waste. However, most of these bosses had little knowledge of music themselves, especially the niche and alternative genres that were in high demand among young rock fans. To maximize their profits, they hired music enthusiasts like me to help them identify valuable albums – those that were popular in underground music circles or had a growing market demand.

I worked for one such boss in Chaoyang Village, Shantou, in 1999, selecting the most valuable tapes for resale. The business quickly became very profitable. With a steady supply of discarded Western music and virtually no acquisition costs other than labour, these small bosses amassed considerable wealth within a few years. Many of them built houses, bought cars, and enjoyed a lifestyle far beyond what factory work could provide.

In the mid-1990s, *Dakou* cassettes were sold in bulk to record shops in Guangzhou, with prices ranging from 300 to 500 CNY per box. Retailers then resold them individually for 5 to 20 CNY, while rare albums – such as Nirvana's – could fetch up to 80 CNY or more. The influence of music magazines also drove market prices. My boss once lamented that he had unknowingly destroyed so many Nirvana tapes – enough to buy a house.

By the early 2000s, however, the *Dakou* trade was in decline. CDs replaced cassettes, but *Dakou* CDs often damaged players, reducing their appeal. The rise of the internet further disrupted the market, making Western music more accessible through piracy and digital downloads.

[End of transcript]

The *Dakou* circuit itself – comprising plastic waste imports, small-scale entrepreneurs, and dedicated Chinese music fans – serves as a broader symbol of the typical consumerist society and reveals one facet of colonial modernity. Here, the discarded cultural products of the West became a spiritual treasure for marginalised Chinese youth. Tapes and CDs once deemed 'unwanted waste' by the global North found new life as cultural gems in the global South represented by the 1990s mainland China. In the end, the *Dakou* business, though primarily economic, reveals the lingering effects of the imbalance of resources and cultural capital between the global North and South.

While *Dakou* cassettes filled a cultural void in China, their arrival was accidental, the by-product of global industrial processes rather than a direct response to Chinese demand. Yet for the young Chinese music fans who made up the '*Dakou* generation', these tapes represented a lifeline to the outside world – a way to connect with global youth culture while living in a rapidly changing and often oppressive social environment.

The Chinese government eventually banned the import of plastic waste in 2018, officially closing the chapter on the *Dakou* trade (Uhm, 2021). By then, however, the internet had long since replaced the need for physical media as the primary source of music discovery.

In summary, the *Dakou* business, which emerged spontaneously in the late 1990s in China, disrupted the established norms of the global music industry by accident. Initially dismissed as waste, these tapes and CDs became a vehicle for cultural exchange and self-education for a generation of Chinese youth. Through their accidental encounters with Western music, the '*Dakou* generation' constructed a new musical identity outside the conventional pathways established by record companies, often dominated by the logic of the market economy. In the years before the rise of the internet, *Dakou* vendors and fans became the curators of an accidental cultural revolution, shaping the musical tastes of a generation through their haphazard collection of cassettes and CDs. Until today, the legacy of the '*Dakou* generation' remains a testament to the power of accidental subversion in the face of domestic restriction and global forces beyond their control.

'*Dakou* generation': Self-education 'with a cut'

> I firmly believe this: 'we must learn to experience all the times of the world in one hour'. For me, Dakou was something that could give me the opportunity to 'experience all the times of the world' in one hour.
>
> – Qiu Dali 邱大立 (Famous music critic and cultural activist, formerly involved in the *Dakou* business)

> I've never sought to mystify *Dakou*. For me, it has simply been a unique way of engaging with the world. The '*Dakou* generation' is one marked by a deep hunger and thirst for diverse music and information – a generation of both scarcity and boundless potential. Many of those who emerged from this era have since become pillars of today's music industry. *Dakou* shouldn't just be viewed as a concept; rather, it represents a tenacity embodied in the relentless pursuit of music.[20]
>
> – Hongfeng 红枫 (Owner of NEWBEE Records, formerly involved in the Dakou business)

The value of *Dakou* cassettes and CDs went beyond economic profit; they had a profound cultural impact, particularly in the formation of the so-called *Dakou* generation (打口一代) in China. This new imaginary urban community, known as the '*Dakou* generation', which emerged on the periphery of Chinese cities in the late twentieth century, consisted of a minority group of urban youth who stood apart from the so-called mainstream Chinese youth. They are scattered across the major cities. Since the 2000s, they have been connected by music bands, underground performances in specific venues, and early online forums. They had a similar passion for rock and alternative music, as well as cinema or other cultural forms from around the world, sharing some common characteristics and seeking new values: personal freedom, authentic self-expression, sexual liberation, and greater social and gender equality. These aspirations deviated from the dominant values imposed by the Chinese authorities through official discourse, educational institutions, and the family order, as well as from the commodification of artistic creation and the market logic brought about by the emerging music and entertainment industries and foreign investment.

In the socio-cultural landscape of 1990s China, dominant values were shaped by state policies promoting the construction of a 'new socialist culture' (社会主义新文化) and the creation of a 'new socialist citizen' (社会主义新人). These concepts were central to the ideological project of the CCP, which sought to build a 'harmonious society' (和谐社会) – a notion based on Confucian ideals of social order and Marxist-Leninist principles of economic reform (Choukroune and Garapon, 2007). Although scholars have criticised this ideology for justifying social control and suppressing dissent, the notion of a 'harmonious society' has remained a cornerstone of CCP policy both at home and abroad. Finally, some scholars also argue that China's own tradition of thinking about harmony can help theorise how the state's soft power can be exercised in less antagonistic and violent ways compared to previous counterparts using similar notions as the ideological core of their power-building, especially the liberal capitalist nation-states such as the United States and Japan (Hagström and Nordin, 2020).

In contrast to the set of dominant values mentioned above, *Dakou* CDs introduced Chinese youth to another world – one of music and culture that was 'illegal' and filled with everything that the newly opened China lacked: 'freedom', 'rebellion', passion, love, and individuality. Chinese rock critic Yan Jun coined the term '*Dakou* generation' to describe those born between the mid-1970s and mid-1980s who came of age between 1990 and 2010. These young people were drawn to the underground culture that emerged through *Dakou* cassettes of rock and alternative music as well as some publications related to the subculture from the West. They shared a sense of belonging that defined their alternative identities in the 1990s. As other critics, musicians, and fans adopted the term '*Dakou* youth' (打口青年), it became a powerful self-identifier for those who rejected mainstream culture.

During this period, China's popular music market was dominated by Hong Kong and Taiwanese pop songs and 'mainstream melodies' (主旋律), which were propagated by the state media and designed to convey the party's ideology. However, this music had little relevance to the real lives of many Chinese youth. Against this backdrop, the circulation of *Dakou* cassettes and CDs, however, helped to foster a marginal community rooted in a shared interest in rock and alternative music and united by the 'underground' attitude and a certain countercultural narrative. For the '*Dakou* generation', these recordings provided their first exposure to Western music, particularly alternative and rock genres.

For the Chinese youth who embraced them, the cassettes or CDs 'with a cut' were a lifeline to the outside world. They connected with global culture while navigating a rapidly changing and at times repressive social landscape. In this sense, the *Dakou* trade has shaped not only the history of rock and alternative music in China but also the personal histories of those who participated in this underground economy, shaped indirectly by global social and economic factors.

However, the relationship between the '*Dakou* generation' and the music was fragmented. The *Dakou* cassettes or CDs were often partially damaged, leading to unpredictable listening experiences – songs skipped, albums played out of order, and so on. Meanwhile, collecting these cassettes or CDs meant accepting whatever happened to be available in secret boxes in a few record shops among the *Dakou* circuit in major cities across China. And yet this randomness became a form of self-education. Fans pieced together their understanding of Western music through a non-linear, often disjointed, and completely 'out of context and reference' process. This chaotic mode of learning mirrored the music they consumed, shaping the *Dakou* generation's unique approach to both global rock culture and self-discovery. Ultimately, their knowledge of music and identity formation was always 'with a cut', embodying their fractured but passionate pursuit of alternative cultural resources and a better understanding of the 'authentic self' as an individual, and not as a member of the ethical family within the traditional Confucius oriented framework; or as a component of 'work units' or organisations; or as a 'model citizen' of a 'new socialist nation-state'.

Finally, as someone who belongs to the '*Dakou* generation', looking back today, I recognise that growing up as part of the 'generation with a cut' was more than just a cultural experience – it was a metaphor for my own process of self-becoming. This journey was marked by cultural scarcity, misunderstanding, and excitement about the 'outside world', but often experienced out of context.

By 'cultural scarcity' I am referring in particular to the limited access to global cultural products and influences during the years of my coming of age. This scarcity manifests itself in two ways: materially, in terms of money, equipment, and available information channels; and structurally, through censorship, media restrictions, and the limited choice of officially sanctioned media and other cultural outlets.

The metaphor of self-becoming also reflects the dual nature of my education. On the one hand, there was the official, structured education – carefully crafted and supervised, with little room for questioning. On the other hand, there was an alternative, self-directed education – one that emerged through chance encounters, illegal imports, and exchanges with like-minded peers. This second dimension did not simply coexist with the first; it often stood in direct opposition to it, challenging its narratives, assumptions, and limitations. At times, it even acted as a deconstructive force, unravelling the seemingly solid frameworks imposed by the official system and replacing them with fragmented, unregulated, and deeply personal forms of knowledge.

The contradictory yet constantly intertwined education shaped not only my intellectual development but also the undertone of my adult character, preparing me for a long and uncertain journey of 'going abroad'. It also set the stage for a new cycle of self-rediscovery and integration in the years that followed. My tracing of this process – the ways in which the contradictory educational path shaped my understanding of culture, identity, and personal transformation – will be the focus of Part II of this book.

Interlude

From *Dakou* to the 'new era' – Navigating the spectacle of 'Chinese independent music' and the unfinished journey

> The spectacle is not a set of images, but a social relationship between people mediated by images.
>
> The spectacle is capital to such an extent that it becomes an image.
>
> – Guy Debord (1967:16, 32)
>
> The economy of music would be reduced to the marketing of the universal spectacle of an infinite disco.
>
> – J. Attali (2001:235)

Parallel to the rise of *Dakou* culture and Chinese underground subcultural communities in the late 1990s, the internet arrived in China in 1997, marking the beginning of a fundamental shift in the distribution, consumption, and production of Chinese popular music as a whole since the opening up. In 2008, about a decade after the internet arrived in China, the number of Chinese internet users reached about 298 million, about a quarter of China's population, reflecting the rapid growth of internet penetration in China. By December 2023, the number of Chinese internet users had skyrocketed to 1.09 billion (CNNIC, 2008; 2024). This radical shift diminished the once important physical network of traditional media such as music magazines, radio and TV programmes, the fan club, record shops including the 'uncensored' *Dakou*, and the circulation of pirated music, as online platforms took control, leading to the gradual disappearance of underground music communities in the outskirts of Beijing.

Meanwhile, since the early 2000s, virtual communities in the form of websites, forums, and chat rooms have flourished, replacing the geographically based subcultures of the previous decade. International record companies, encouraged by the economic reforms of the 1990s, also began to enter the country. The combination of foreign capital and local investment fostered the rapid growth of a relatively complete music industry infrastructure by the early twenty-first century. As a result, the once marginalised and underground scene of Chinese rock and alternative music, deeply influenced and imbued with the myths of revolutionary rock and the 'subversive, anti-commercial' underground, was gradually absorbed by the forces of commercialisation and commodification, following a trajectory familiar to other global music circuits.

In summary, at the dawn of the new millennium, the rise of the internet facilitated the exchange of music and information among Chinese youth, as well as the globalisation of the Chinese popular music industry. It also had a profound impact on the multiple myths about rock, *Yaogun*, and 'underground music' that had emerged due to the scarcity of music resources and the lack of development of the music industry, as well as the interpretation/misinterpretation of some key figures in the Chinese cultural and musical landscape through words during the 1990s. As a result, the rhetoric of revolution and subversion that characterised *Yaogun* throughout the 1990s began to fade among the new generation of musicians. Movements such as Modern Sky Records and the New Sound of Beijing embodied this shift, distancing themselves from the earlier generation of 'cultural heroes'. In general, these newer iterations of *Yaogun* were more pragmatic, more fun, and more focused on everyday, personal life than the 'greater causes' that reflected collective concerns or aspirations. With the help of critics and the new media – internet – a new label of 'Chinese independent music' was established, and the 'glory of Chinese rock' gradually faded in the musical landscape of the new millionaires.

According to the French social theorist Guy Debord (1967), spectacle is a social relationship mediated by appearances and images that replaces reality with representation; this concept of spectacle was used to criticise the alienation of people's everyday lives in Western capitalist societies in the 1960s. From today's perspective, however, Debord's concept accurately captures the essence of the profound changes in Chinese society in the 1990s. In China's 'new era', *Yaogun* and 'Chinese independent music' became entangled in a labyrinth of images and symbols, reflecting the cultural fragmentation that Debord observed in Western society some 30 years ago.

In the realm of Chinese rock music, apart from the emergence and impact of the internet, the emergence of music festivals in China at the turn of the millennium also marked a significant cultural shift. The first major Chinese rock festival – the Midi Music Festival (迷笛音乐节) – debuted in 2000 and was soon followed by others across the country. By the end of the first decade of the twenty-first century, more than 100 music festivals had sprung up across China, reflecting the 'synchronicity of Chinese culture' with the global rise of open-air music events thanks to communication technology. These festivals represented both a freer political and social atmosphere and the commodification of Chinese independent music, which became a cultural product linking China's emerging middle class with global lifestyle trends, while also confirming the reality of the 'reoccupation of Chinese rock' by market logic and the fate of its commodification after the economic and social transformation of the 1990s. By 2025 corporate media will be talking about 'the rise of music festivals in Asia' from a marketing perspective, as the statistics of predicted profits take precedence over the ideal of 'rejuvenating Chinese culture' or the pursuit of an ideal myth about 'music changing lives' or 'rock against the established order' (Bradley, 2024).

In a way, the explosion of music festivals in the new millennium reflects how the label of 'Chinese independent music' – which encompasses both rock and alternative music – has been transformed into something comparable to mainstream pop. Once positioned in opposition to mainstream pop and central to the myth of *Yaogun* as a countercultural force, both rock and alternative music have now blurred that distinction. Today, 'independent music' and mainstream pop share similar commercial implications, making the once-clear boundaries between them increasingly ambiguous.

In conclusion, the proliferation of music festivals in China underscores the convergence of cultural and economic forces in the 'new era'. While the rise of these festivals reflects a more open and flexible political and social atmosphere, it also illustrates the deepening commercialisation of 'Chinese independent music', or all forms of modern Chinese culture in general. From Cui Jian to the music festival boom, from a vehicle of individual and collective voice to a symbol of lifestyle, the trajectory of Chinese rock represents the complex interplay of politics, economics, and artistic expression of a cultural phenomenon that is uniquely situated in the context of modern China. However, it also reveals the tricky journey of 'identity search and integration' that cannot be separated from the global context and the current framework of cultural imperialism.

In the end, this interrogation of Chinese rock mirrors my own journey of identity search, self-finding, re-finding, and integration. Researching Chinese rock has not only been an academic endeavour but also a deeply personal exploration, intertwining with my experiences of moving across different cultural and geographical landscapes – from my hometown to Beijing, then from Beijing to France, and finally from France to the United Kingdom. Each transition reshaped my self-perception and challenged my understanding of both my own cultural background and the Western societies I encountered.

In this journey, I have moved, both physically and intellectually, from the 'margin' to the 'centre' (hooks, 1984), only to find that the centre itself is not a fixed point but a construct shaped by power, history, and various perspectives. From the 'centre', I returned to the 'margin' – not simply in a geographical sense, but in the realisation that each new environment repositioned what I had previously perceived as the 'centre'. What once seemed like a point of arrival or authority became decentred, revealing new margins, new peripheries, and new questions. In this constant process of reorientation, I found myself shifting between frameworks of belonging and estrangement, renegotiating my understanding of cultural identity. Part II will explore this trajectory in greater depth, tracing how these movements shaped not only my academic inquiries but also my evolving sense of self in relation to the cultural and ideological forces at play.

PART II
Cross-cultural identity in motion: Navigating the journey from 'me' to 'us'

EVERTHING BEGINS BY LEAVING

People always ask about beginning. We strive after newness, the shiny, the acquisition of possibility. A proxy for our own longing to begin anew on the journey of finding ourselves because we haven't yet gotten there. What we don't often ask is, 'What made me choose me?' and 'What had to end?' and 'What got left behind?'

– A. K. Williams *et al.* (2016: 25)

6
Leaving home: From Kunming to Beijing – The awareness of centre and periphery

In the summer of 2001, about three years after discovering the world of *Yaogun* and rock, I graduated from the high school in Kunming with a high score in the *gaokao* – the fiercely competitive national entrance exam that determines whether students can enter top universities based on their grades. My results earned me a place at Peking University, one of China's top institutions – the Oxford/Cambridge of the United Kingdom or the Harvard of the United States. With this achievement came the pride of my parents, extended family and friends, as well as a great deal of expectation and pressure from those around me, especially as the 'only child' of the family, and as the only grandchild to have ever been so 'successful' in the *gaokao* on either side of my family.

At that time, a degree from Peking University still carried a great deal of weight in China, both in material and social terms. Graduates from elite universities were often rewarded with high-profile jobs and greater opportunities, especially during the accelerating period of social change in the late 1990s and early 2000s, while education itself – highly valued in Chinese tradition – conferred social respect. Everyone around me expected me to go on and secure a prestigious position in the big city, earn a high salary, and bring honour to my family. By the early 2000s, the 'prestigious position' and the collective perception of 'success' had already shifted considerably from the 'traditional/socialist Chinese narrative', in which personal worth is very much measured by social/political status and the collective moral evaluation of one's surroundings. In the new century, in addition to conventional values such as social/political status 'within the system', one's reputation in one's surroundings and the wider collective environment, the idea of success was also heavily influenced by the rapid economic development of the market economy. Under the advertisements and promises of the new media and the 'international, modernised' narrative, the emerging urban Chinese affluent class now had a new model of the 'successful good life', encapsulated in the 'Chinese Dream' – a vision of prosperity that blended economic success with social harmony. This ideal promoted a life with a high-paying job, a nice house, a car, and a nuclear family with lovely children, yet remained deeply rooted in Confucian traditions, valuing the presence of extended family. In essence, it was an adapted image of typical middle-class life in a developed capitalist society, where personal worth was increasingly measured by economic gain and materialist standards, but still infused with cultural ideals of collective well-being and national rejuvenation (Bislev, 2015).

As someone who listened to rock music and began to look at the world around me with a somewhat sceptical eye, I found the dominant narrative of the 'successful life' – the blending of the Chinese Dream with the American Dream – less appealing. However, I was also looking forward to university life, with the anticipation of finally escaping the monotony of high school, which had been filled with endless studying, mock exams, and homework, with almost no entertainment or social life.

More than that, I was eager to leave behind the familiar but boring environment of the residential blocks where I grew up – an auxiliary housing area of a military hospital where both my parents worked; where twice a day the loudspeaker in the compound played the wake-up call and the lunch break call; where everyone knew everyone else and their family members because they lived in the same building and worked together in the hospital several hundred metres away during the day; where private, public, and professional lives intermingled seamlessly; and where everyone wore the same uniform, followed the same pattern, and accepted it as if it had to be so, without question.

I was also eager to leave my hometown of Kunming, a lovely place with nice weather, delicious food, diverse ethnical culture, and a relaxed lifestyle, but which seemed provincial compared to bustling and 'cosmopolitan' cities like Beijing and Shanghai, especially for an 18-year-old young girl who had discovered the alternative voices through *Yaogun* and rock. I was eager to see something new and different, places where people were not just worried about three meals a day and were working, resting, or engaging in the daily rhythm of neighbourhood gossip – a common pastime where everyone knew each other, and the lines between personal, private, and public lives blurred. I yearned for something beyond the mundane routines and the anticipation of the 'glorious future' of the younger generations. Especially after developing a whole set of romantic imaginations about the world of rock music and the 'free spirit' inspired by the articles and radio programmes I listened to – as a rare escape during my high school days. Most of all, I longed to finally leave home to 'find myself', echoing the sentiments of so many rock songs I had listened to, although I wasn't quite sure what my 'true self' meant at that time. Nevertheless, I left Kunming and began a new chapter of my life in the early 2000s in Beijing – the political and cultural capital of the PRC.

Peking University's campus is located on Beijing's 4th Ring Road in the northwest of Beijing city, adjacent to Tsinghua University, another top-ranked university, and several other prestigious Chinese universities and research institutes. The area, known as Wudaokou (五道口), had played a significant role in shaping Beijing's cultural landscape in the early 2000s, particularly in terms of education, international influence, and urban development. The large student population, including many international students, creates a vibrant intellectual atmosphere, making Wudaokou a unique cultural melting pot within Beijing.

In the early 2000s, Wudaokou also became a breeding ground for renowned bars and live venues within the rock and underground music scene. In addition to the vibrant cultural scene, the area also includes Zhongguancun （中关村）, a major technology hub often referred to as China's Silicon Valley. Zhongguancun's rise to prominence began in the 1980s when it was designated as one of China's first technology parks. It was an intriguing juxtaposition.

In retrospect, Wudaokou in the early 2000s represented a unique, dynamic microcosm within Beijing, combining education, international influences, technology and urban development, and emerging subculture. It played a crucial role in Beijing's rock and alternative music scene at the beginning of the new twenty-first century, as many of the Chinese underground bands that emerged in the late 1990s had their first performances in Wudaokou's bars and venues. Also in this area, several bookshops and record stores have become famous among alternative culture and music lovers for selling Western philosophical books – ranging from Enlightenment thought to a large selection of modern French and German works on Romanticism to Existentialism, modern ethics, modernism, post-modernism, and related topics – as well as *Dakou* audiovisual products, which were available behind the closed doors. It was during my four years at Peking University that I began to attend rock concerts and experience live music. Therefore, Peking University and Wudaokou became a kind of 'second spiritual home' for me, where I studied, loved, laughed and cried, dreamt, and got lost, where I immersed myself in countless live performances, where I spent sleepless nights with friends who shared the same passion, leaving an unforgettable mark on my twenties.

Awareness of centre and periphery

Back to the year 2001, when I had just gotten the results of the *gaokao* and was admitted to Peking University to study Chinese language and literature. I was filled with pride and excitement, considered a top student from Kunming city, and congratulated by all my friends, teachers, and relatives. Coming from the capital of Yunnan Province, I had worked hard to earn my place at one of China's most prestigious institutions (Peking University admitted only five students from Yunnan in Humanities and Social Sciences out of more than 300,000 students who took the *gaokao* in 2001). However, it didn't take long for me to feel the huge gap between myself and many of my classmates who came from more central and developed cities and regions such as Beijing, Shanghai, Hubei, Hunan, Shandong, and Guangdong.

This divide wasn't just economic – although that was certainly part of it – but also cultural, informational, and educational. As students of Chinese language and literature, reading a large number of classical Chinese texts was a fundamental requirement. While my peers were immersed in Chinese classical texts and literature from an early age – often supported by family and regional traditions, private tutors, and additional resources beyond the standard curriculum – my own experience was limited to a few extracts from standard textbooks in the national curriculum at school. Discussions in class and in the dormitory (we were six girls sharing a small dormitory at the time) often left me feeling disoriented as my classmates, all elite students from all over the country, seemed to have already mastered material that was completely new to me. I became very close to another girl from Guizhou Province – another 'remote' province in southwest China, which was considered 'poor and backward' in comparison to the 'central areas', much like my home area of Yunnan – because we shared a similar feeling of being left behind by our classmates.

The anxiety and sense of marginalisation I felt in those early days were overwhelming. For the first time, I began to doubt my abilities and question whether I really belonged in such an environment. At the same time, my self-esteem took a hit as I struggled to keep up with the conversations and studies that my peers were navigating with ease.

However, this experience marked a crucial turning point in my understanding of the world. With a huge sense of contrast and a feeling of 'falling out' after the brief, glorious bubble period following the *gaokao*, I began to see the deep systemic inequalities rooted in geography, politics, and economics. The unbalanced distribution of resources based on where one was born and raised became apparent, as did the concept of a centre and a periphery within a society. It wasn't just about ability, personal effort, and education; it was also about a wider structural injustice that shaped lives in profound ways.

In retrospect, this realisation was crucial. It exposed me to the pressures of the dominant group and the powerful influence of structural power dynamics on individual self-perception. It was in those moments of struggle and self-doubt that I first began to understand the complex interplay between power, privilege, and identity – a lesson that would continue to shape my perspective and academic journey. It was also against this backdrop that I began to find my 'alternative cohort' in the student societies on campus – a community of marginalised students from all disciplines and backgrounds who came together under the label of 'rock 'n' roll', a group of 'misfit' students who shared a passion for rock music and a desire to be 'authentic' and 'rebellious', and who were influenced by all the myths that the label of rock or

Yaogun still carried in the early 2000s. It was also where I began to find a 'real connection' and a sense of belonging throughout my time at university in Beijing.

Feeling 'free and alive': First gig in the suburbs of Beijing

My first experience of attending a *Yaogun* gig took me far beyond the sense of being an 'outsider' that I had felt at Peking University. It made me feel connected to the city in a way that transcended the isolation and distance I had experienced among my peers. It was shortly after I entered university that I attended an underground night at a venue called *Haoyun* (豪运酒吧) – one of Beijing's first live venues for rock, especially 'heavy music' (this place no longer exists). I was invited by a classmate, a passionate metalhead from Beijing, who was familiar with the venues and concert information. The venue was on the 4th Ring Road in the eastern part of the city, and it took us almost three hours by bus to get there. This was my first live gig ever; I was both excited and nervous.

There were several heavy metal bands in the line-up that night, including some bands that became famous in the underground music circles in the mid-2000s. The event started at around 10 pm and went on until 3 am. As we entered the dimly lit venue, I was struck by the crowd – almost entirely male. I was probably one of only three or four women in the whole audience. My classmate (a man), probably not sensing my nervousness and discomfort, simply told me to 'have fun' before leaving me alone and disappearing into the crowd.

However, driven by a mixture of excitement and curiosity – much like the first time I followed an unknown guy to buy the *Dakou* cassette in a secret place – I rushed to the front row where the most ardent fans had gathered. Surrounded by a sea of men, all jumping and pushing each other to the rhythm of the heavy music, I felt a wave of fear at first. Being small and slight, I was terrified of falling and being trampled. But within minutes, the raw energy and passion of the crowd had completely captured me. I started jumping with them, shaking my head like crazy, even pushing some guys back, swept up in the wild, exhilarating chaos – later I learnt that this particular type of audience movement during live rock concerts was called *pogo*.

When the gig ended at 3 am, I finally found my classmate. We were both exhausted. He had lost his mobile phone – a luxury item for students in the early 2000s – but his spirits were high. As we stepped out into the biting winter air, with almost no one on the street and our breath rising in white clouds of mist, my friend threw his head back and shouted to the sky, 'Life!'

I've long since forgotten how we managed to get back to campus that night. But that scene – standing on the 4th Ring Road in eastern Beijing at 3 am, surrounded by darkness, cold air, and the lingering thrill of the gig – remains vivid in my memory. Despite the exhaustion, the mix of emotions, and the biting cold, I felt a powerful sensation: this was 'real life'.

After that night, I started attending every underground music concert I could find in Beijing with my fellow rock enthusiasts from the 'Peking University Rock Music Society'. Most of the gigs were held in the Wudaokou area near Peking University, where several venues became famous for hosting rock gigs during the first decade of the 2000s. Many late nights followed, marked by the ritual of walking back to the dormitory after midnight, with no one around but 'rock fellows', with beer and cigarette in hand, feeling completely exhausted but deeply happy, free, and, above all, 'alive'.

'Last utopia': Midi Music Festival

The 2002 Midi Music Festival (迷笛音乐节) was my first experience of a *Yaogun* music festival, and it left a deep impression on me. It took place during the Chinese May Day holiday, a time when people across the country are eager for a break from work. With my best friend at the time, a girl from the same high school in the city of Kunming, also a rare (female) rock music lover, I embarked on an adventure that felt like a pilgrimage. Having read about Woodstock in music magazines and books, I had a vague idea of what a festival might be like, but I had never had the opportunity to attend one in China, either in Kunming or Beijing. (It turned out that the Midi Music Festival was also the first music festival dedicated to rock and alternative music in mainland China, having started two years earlier to support the graduate students at the music school of the same name.) It was about six months after I'd landed in Beijing and I'd already experienced the excitement of live underground music with my classmate in the suburbs of Beijing, but nothing could have prepared me for what I was about to experience.

The Midi Music Festival was organised by mainland China's first 'modern music' school (focusing on modern music instruments such as electronic guitar, bass, and drums) called Midi Music

Academy（迷笛音乐学校）, which was founded by jazz enthusiast Zhang Fan 张帆 in 1993. Far more than just a celebration of music, it was the first rock and alternative music festival ever held in the PRC and helped shape the landscape of Chinese music festivals afterwards. The festival began in 1999 on the academy's campus, initially as a free event for students to showcase their talents, but quickly evolved into something much more. In 2002, the festival moved outdoors for the first time under a bright May sky. The weather was perfect: not too hot, not too cold for Beijing, with the free-flowing beer in the air. It was a gathering of thousands of 'cool', 'rebellious', or 'non-mainstream' young Chinese – people who in other parts of China might be considered 'outsiders' or 'misfits', but here they were united by a shared passion for music, an 'independent and free spirit', and a common yearning for 'being true to yourself'.

I still remember arriving at the festival and being in awe – so many young, cool, 'alternative', and free-spirited people, all so radically different from anything I had seen before. People with punk haircuts, dyed hair, tattoos, leather pants, and heavy necklaces – girls among them, with cigarettes in hand and bold, provocative outfits. Meanwhile, on both sides of the road leading up to the entrance, there were a lot of local people – many of them farmers from the suburbs and manual laborers, who didn't know much about *Yaogun*, but who realised that it was a good business opportunity As a result, thousands of Chinese rock lovers were strangely mingled with local people who had stalls selling street food and local snacks, and were happy to look at these 'strange young people' with curiosity. There was a mix of all kinds of people from totally different social, cultural, and educational backgrounds here, in the middle of nowhere on the 5th Ring Road of eastern Beijing, connecting in a strange, lively, yet harmonious way. As someone who grew up with labels such as 'good student', 'dutiful daughter', and 'model young girl' in the eyes of my family, friends, and relatives, I felt for a brief moment so 'normal', almost boring, compared to these cool young Chinese. But that feeling didn't last long as I was swept up in the energy of the festival. It was unlike anything I had ever experienced: thousands of people gathered around a shared passion – they probably had the same sense of being on the margins of all sorts of 'centres' in society but were very excited and happy to be there, with many of them getting drunk before the music even started, sitting on the grass, laughing, and preparing for what felt like a communal release.

The fresh, raw, carnival-like atmosphere of the Midi Festival set the standard for music festivals throughout China, which quickly flourished in the following decades. It also became an important symbol of what a 'real festival' was for many people who attended its early versions. The early Midi Festivals featured several bands such as Muma (木马), Painful Faith (痛苦的信仰), Coldblooded Animals (冷血动物), Tongue (舌头), and Ruins (废墟) – groups that would become the backbone of Chinese rock for years to come, many of whom remain prominent and have become the 'icons of *Yaogun*' today. In a way, the Midi Music Academy and its festival paved the way for the 'festival boom' in the contemporary Chinese music industry. From music education and networking to providing the first stages for emerging young musicians, Midi definitely played a foundational role.

Looking back at the Midi Music Festival of 2002, for 19-year-old me, it was a peak experience – one that would always remain somewhere in my memory. For the first time I discovered the magic power of music to evoke a subtle and soft part of the human heart hidden under the 'heavy and hard' outlook. Despite the 'rawness' of rock music – heavy and aggressive, accompanied by screaming vocals and pounding guitars – the atmosphere at the 2002 Midi Festival was strangely warm. People who seemed angry, bumping into each other during the music in what I later came to understand as *pogo*, were friendly and open when the music stopped. It was as if we were part of a larger family, united by a shared love of music, of 'freedom', and of being together in the moment, everyone just being happy, human beings, not carrying the weights of different social labels (family role, having a diploma, social status, regional background, etc.) that seem to separate us and make us feel stressed. Even the locals (mostly workers and farmers from nearby villages) who had set up stalls selling snacks and cigarettes, who were not really interested in heavy and noisy music, revelled in the festival atmosphere, perhaps not fully understanding the music but enjoying the sense of collective joy.

For me personally, the Midi Festival, at least in its early years, was a gathering that carried the weight of a group of young people's hopes, frustrations, and desires for liberation. It was a rare space where young people came together to celebrate life, to push back against rigid social norms, and to experience a fleeting yet intoxicating sense of freedom. For a brief moment, the festival allowed an escape from collective dogmatism, family expectations, and the relentless pressures of an increasingly competitive, meritocratic society.

Beyond its role as a site of rebellion and celebration, the festival also embodied a raw, unfiltered energy that reflected the spirit of its time. The uninhibited attitudes of the attendees – gathering for relaxation, revelry, and catharsis – created a space of genuine expression. This spirit resonated deeply with the myths of rock and *Yaogun* that had been established by early Chinese media and broadcasting, myths that had captivated young audiences like me. The early Midi Festival became a living embodiment of those ideals – a place where the rebellious and liberating ethos of rock music felt tangibly alive.

But it was also a utopia that quickly faded. As Chinese society moved into a more market-driven and entertainment-oriented era, the festival began to change. The so-called festival boom saw events increasingly sponsored by corporations and in collaboration with local authorities, often with the aim of promoting tourism and stimulating the economy. The raw, chaotic energy of the early years gave way to a more polished, commercialised version of the festival, marking the end of an era.

In the end, the Midi Festival, once a symbol of youthful revelry, celebration, and idealistic escape, became a reflection of wider changes in Chinese society, where profit and marketability began to overshadow the spirit of rebellion, liberation, and pure fun that had defined its origins.

Today it seems almost unimaginable that a music festival could be held with thousands of people in attendance and with free, unlimited beer, but back then the festival operated on an idealism that hadn't yet been overtaken by market logic. In fact, 2002 was the last time free beer was offered at Midi, and it feels like the last time such idealism could exist, not just for the festival, but for the broader context of youth culture in China. The Midi Festival of the early 2000s was a product of its time – a utopia that briefly flourished in a world that had yet to be fully commodified. I've read in many media reports and interviews that Zhang Fan's vision for the Midi Festival was not just about promoting music; it was about fostering a space where young people could gather, be themselves, and express themselves without the constraints of society weighing them down. I would say that the 2002 Midi Festival actually realised this, at least for me. When I think back to that time, I realise how lucky I was to have lived through it.

Years later, after I had moved to Europe, I understood how rare and incredible that moment was. It was a fleeting bubble of idealism, much like Woodstock – a space born out of a unique set of social circumstances that couldn't last. The Midi festival of those years was an expression of youth, 'freedom', and rebellion against the backdrop of a rapidly changing China. Though another Woodstock may never happen in China, what the Midi Festival offered in its early years was something spiritually similar – a moment of purity, however subjective, where music and idealism converged, and where thousands of Chinese young people found a sense of belonging in their shared defiance of the norm and simply 'being themselves', in the PRC.

Home and identity

Leaving home was more than just a physical journey for me; it marked the beginning of my journey towards self-discovery and independence. Growing up in Kunming, my sense of self was inextricably linked to my childhood environment – the military hospital compound, my family, my neighbours, and the shared routines of daily life. Everyone around me was caught in a web of expectations defined by family roles and social obligations. Leaving home for Peking University allowed me to take the first steps towards unravelling these threads, providing the distance I needed to question who I really was, beyond inherited roles and expectations.

In Chinese society, this process of breaking free from collective expectations was particularly significant. It has been shaped by centuries of Confucian values intertwined with socialist ideals and narratives. In this context, the individual is positioned within a web of responsibilities defined by obligations to family, community, workplace, and the state – a framework in which personal identity is often subordinated to collective obligations. The Confucian concept of *Jun-Chen Fu-Zi* (君臣父子), roughly translated as 'Ruler and Subject, Father and Son', defined the hierarchy of relationships that formed the core of social identity – a patriarchal contract in which women played a largely subordinate role. In the context of China's long feudal history, although Mao's revolution and socialist narratives severely challenged many aspects of this contract, it didn't change its core.

During the revolutionary era, women were 'liberated' and considered 'equal' to men. They were given the same opportunities in the workplace and took on the same responsibilities as their male counterparts, but they still had to fulfil their 'duties' as 'wives and daughters' at home, as the family structure and hierarchies were hardly touched and challenged from within. At the time, however, I was blind to the oppressive nature of this framework, especially in terms of gender roles – a realisation that only became clear to me years later, after living abroad.

Leaving home provided the physical, mental, and geographical distance I needed to explore the possibility of 'self' as an independent entity, not just a dutiful daughter, a 'model student', or an aspiring high achiever. Yet those four years at university were anything but an exciting and painful journey of self-discovery. As much as leaving home offered a sense of relative freedom, I often found myself feeling lost, overwhelmed by the gap between my upbringing and the experiences of my classmates – all high achievers from more 'developed' regions. This gap wasn't just material but also cultural and experiential. While I prided myself on my knowledge of rock music, alternative cultural expressions, and independent thinking, these passions seemed almost irrelevant in the highly competitive environment of Peking University, where academic excellence and conventional success often took precedence. It felt like everything I held dear had lost its meaning, overshadowed by new and intimidating standards, with explicit benchmarks and references to mark your value and achievements.

Amid this sense of alienation, I found my community – not the one defined by residential blocks, extended family, or classmates bound by circumstance, but a community I actively sought and chose. The Rock Music Society at Peking University, along with online alternative music radios and forums, became my refuge – a space where a small group of students and anonymous listeners gathered to share our love of rock and alternative voices, seeking something beyond the dominant narrative of achievement and status. In different ways, we were all 'outsiders', marginalised within the university and broader social contexts.

It was in these spaces – through late-night discussions, online exchanges, and the raw energy of live gigs – that I discovered a sense of belonging. The Rock Music Society, online music forums, and the Midi Festival together formed a collective space where hierarchies and social pressures momentarily dissolved, where idealism could breathe, and where I felt at home.

Looking back, it was in those moments – at rock gigs or lying on the grass at the Midi Music Festival – that I began to form my personal and cultural identity. It was an identity rooted in ideals of equality, freedom, compassion, and hope for a more diverse, tolerant, and 'enlightened society'. These beliefs were deeply influenced by my reading of philosophical thinkers, especially the translated works of European, and in particular French, scholars, and the myth of an 'Enlightened Europe', which resonated closely with the myth of rock and *Yaogun* that I deeply cherished at the time through these readings. It was this idealism that inspired me to continue my studies in France after my time at Peking University – a decision that would lead to new revelations and disillusionments.

7
Departing China for France: The second move and the disillusionment of an 'enlightened Europe'

> All human truth is an optical illusion….the truth is always in the turning point, where it reverses itself.
>
> – Søren Kierkegaard (1847, in Dru 1959: 618)

Leaving China for France was not unlike leaving Kunming; it marked a new chapter in my life – a second profound departure on my journey of self-discovery. But this time it was more than just physical and mental distance from my immediate family and social environment – it was a leap of faith into an imaginary world, driven by a longing for something I had only glimpsed in books and translated works.

When I decided to continue my studies in France after completing my BA at Peking University, I had already been learning French and preparing for this transition for some time. My mother had mixed feelings about my choice. On one hand, she saw the value of going abroad – experiencing the wider world, gaining knowledge, and living in another country. Like many Chinese people, she viewed France as a land of romance, freedom, and rich cultural heritage. She supported my decision and took pride in my achievement.

My mother had charted her own path of independence. She was the only female soldier selected from her small town near the Vietnamese border and left home at 17 to attend military school in Kunming. In a place where many girls had limited access to education and few opportunities to change their fate, she defied convention. Raised as a 'model student and daughter' under Mao Zedong's socialist ideals of gender equality, she grew into an intellectual, ambitious, and resilient woman. Over the years, she built a successful career and achieved social status, embodying her ideals of self-determination and progress.

Her pride in me stemmed from the same aspirations. Like many of her peers who had moved away from a restrictive environment, she valued education and social mobility. My graduation from one of China's top universities and the opportunity to study at a prestigious European institution symbolised success in her eyes. She hoped that I would return with a highly regarded degree, thus reinforcing upward mobility and securing a 'good life'.

Yet, beneath her pride, there was also hesitation. She had already watched me leave home once for Beijing, and now I was heading even further away – to another continent, with a different language and culture, and without the safety net of family or connections. The excitement of new possibilities was shadowed by her deep-seated concern. My departure was not just a step forward in my journey but also marked a widening distance between us – one that she struggled to reconcile.

But it was also partly due to a collective order in the form of a 'common belief' in Chinese society – that a girl doesn't need to pursue education beyond a BA degree (yes, it's important for a girl to get a higher education degree, just like the boy, but no more). Instead, a legacy of Confucius, of ancient imperial feudal patriarchy, has always been there, deeply embedded in the social consciousness and collective mindset of Chinese society, that it is always more important for a girl to find a 'suitable match', settle down with a stable job, and start a family, before a certain biologic age, much more so than for a boy. Getting a master's degree or even higher and achieving high social status with prestigious titles or economic gains are relatively less common expectations for girls, let alone going abroad to do it alone. On the contrary, boys, as the socially constructed gender, have borne the brunt of such family and social expectations, especially in rural parts of China.

At that time, France existed in my mind as an idealised world – a world fundamentally different from the one in which I had grown up. Its language, culture, history, social structures, and spiritual traditions felt not only foreign but, in my imagination, superior – more advanced, more enlightened. My vision of Europe, and of France in particular, was as a beacon of progress and freedom, a land of liberal artists and alternative, free-thinking souls.

I imagined a country that truly embodied the ideals of 'liberté, égalité, fraternité' – a place where creativity and individuality flourished.

The myth and romantic idealism I'd constructed around France began to unravel soon after my arrival. Like the Chinese intellectuals of the 1980s who idealised rock music as a symbol of liberation, I had imagined France as an 'enlightened' utopia. But Lyon, the city where I lived and studied for nearly a decade while completing my PhD on Chinese rock and social transformation, quickly challenged this illusion.

My time there was marked by moments of both revelation and disillusionment. While Lyon offered inspiring personal freedoms, vibrant cultural scenes, and public debates, it also exposed hidden fractures in republican contradictions and colonial echoes – a system grappling with urban riots in the so-called lost territories of the Republic, where marginalised immigrant communities faced systemic neglect that was completely outside my idealised image of the French Republic (Rutkevich, 2023).

Meanwhile, my daily life revealed more subtle tensions: the condescension towards non-Parisian accents that I noticed in conversations, the unspoken bias in social circles and practical tasks, especially when looking for housing and jobs, the weight of France's colonial legacy in how the tension between 'Français de souche' (native French) and French citizens of immigrant descent (particularly Algerian-French citizens) manifested itself in everyday life situations. These experiences forced me to re-examine my own upbringing. Distance from China sharpened my awareness of its internal contradictions – the patriarchal norms masked by socialist rhetoric, the feudal undertones lingering beneath capitalist reforms. Yet Lyon also taught me that such power structures were not unique to China. In France, they wore different masks: Eurocentric assumptions, the quiet dominance of inherited privilege, the friction between republican ideals and racial realities.

Losing labels: From an elite Peking university student to an 'asian', 'female', 'foreigner'

In Beijing, I had internalised the status with prestige that came with being a student at Peking University – something I took for granted. It had given me a kind of respect and recognition within China that automatically marked me as part of the 'elite'. Although I was from Kunming – a place still considered peripheral compared to Beijing – and both my parents came from humble social backgrounds (my mother from a small town near the border with Vietnam, the daughter of a soldier who had joined the 'Red Army' from the northern China during the civil war; my father, the eldest son of peasant parents living in a rudimentary village 60 kilometres from Kunming, one of the basic units of rural China) – I had, in a sense, made my way to the 'centre' by excelling within China's intellectual and social hierarchy.

I felt that the sense of being marginalised on campus was rooted in my personal perception of identity and cultural belonging when compared to many students. Nevertheless, I was still positioned as an 'elite student' in the eyes of Chinese society, and this label afforded me numerous advantages and privileges: access to a vast collection of cultural resources at the Peking University library; affordable and convenient tickets to numerous conferences and performances held on campus; opportunities to meet renowned writers and scholars and interact with them directly; and highly efficient, inexpensive logistical services provided by the university – from affordable student accommodation and canteen on campus and shops, post office, bookstores to a dedicated bank branch that allowed students to apply for credit cards without a credit check. Simply being a Peking University student acted as a form of guarantee. Yet I was largely unaware of these privileges, focusing only on my perceived 'alternative position' and my sense of being lost. But when I arrived in France, the change was so direct, immediate, and jarring. The social values and privileges attached to the labels I had carried for so long, albeit almost unconsciously – labels that once held power – disappeared completely.

Suddenly, my identity was reduced to three factors that seemed so 'unnatural', almost forced upon me: I was 'Asian', 'female', and a 'foreign student from China'. The social credit I had worked so hard to achieve in China meant nothing in my new environment. I was painfully aware that I had entered a much larger 'periphery' – not just as a Chinese girl from a southwestern city who liked rock music but as a 'true outsider', and in many cases, I was a not-so-well-regarded outsider in the Western world.

It's important to highlight the stark contrast in how China and France (and the wider West) have portrayed each other through their media and intellectual discourses. Mainstream Chinese narratives often idealised France as an 'enlightened' beacon of culture and progress. Meanwhile, French and Western media reduced China to two reductive labels: one, an 'ancient China' frozen in time and treated as a relic of history; the other, a 'revolutionary, socialist China', portrayed as totalitarian and oppressive. These contrasting portrayals – China's romanticised view of France and the West's stigmatised view of China – revealed more about the biases of the observers than the observed.

For the West, China became a foil for the 'liberal, democratic' ideal, dismissed as archaic or authoritarian. Conversely, Chinese narratives portrayed France as a utopian counterpoint to their own developing society. This mutual oversimplification reflected broader global divisions: individuals from the global South migrating to the North were labelled 'immigrants', while those moving in the opposite direction became 'expatriates'. Such distinctions, often shaped by media and state rhetoric, reinforced hierarchies that reduced complex societies to ideological caricatures and often emphasize division and conflict.

As music scholar Michael L. Jones (2008) observes of Josephine Baker's career in Paris: 'Baker's experience as a 'Black American in Paris'... proceeded only as and through one or more stereotypes' (Jones, 2008: 714). Like Baker, I found myself navigating France as an Asian student limited by reductive labels. Before China's global image shifted with the 2008 Olympics, my identity in France was flattened into tropes of the 'Asian/Chinese female student' – a figure expected to learn, improve, or even 'liberate' herself through exposure to the West. In the popular imagination, this arc might culminate in marrying a 'rich Frenchman' or securing systemic privileges.

Stripped of the social capital my achievements in Beijing had afforded me, I became invisible in a society where the dominance of Western media and narrow representations of 'diversity' left little room for nuanced identities. The same curiosity and intellect that defined me at Peking University were overshadowed by assumptions about my race and gender. Institutional indifference compounded this erasure: in seminars, my perspectives were met with polite detachment; in social circles, I was exoticised or overlooked.

France's 'enlightened' ideals, I realised, coexisted with a structural stigmatisation of outsiders. Like Baker, I existed in a paradox: hypervisible as a stereotype yet erased as an individual. The marginalisation I'd felt in China resurfaced here, but now magnified by Eurocentric hierarchies. Where Beijing's restrictions were familiar, France's liberal facade made its exclusions harder to name – and infinitely lonelier to confront.

Eurocentrism unveiled: The myth of Enlightenment cracks

Before my trip to France, my image of Europe – shaped by the myth of rock, *Yaogun*, and the Enlightenment narratives I'd consumed in China – was one of intellectual freedom and moral progress. Like many of my peers, I idealised Enlightenment thought itself: its celebration of reason, human rights, and social justice, epitomised by France but rooted in a broader European heritage that included British and German philosophy. For me, these ideals transcended borders to form the ethical bedrock of modernity. France in particular stood as a beacon, its revolutionary history and human rights rhetoric positioning it as the vanguard of dignity and equality. This uncritical admiration, however, overlooked the contradictions embedded in Enlightenment universalism – flaws that I would later come to confront not only in France but across Europe.

My first few months in Lyon (the city where I successfully secured a place to study and the place where I finally landed in France) shattered the Enlightenment illusion quickly. My first accommodation was in a public housing complex in the suburbs – an HLM (Habitation à Loyer Modéré). HLM or 'low rent housing' refers to a system of public or subsidised housing. It is designed to provide affordable accommodations for individuals and families with limited financial means. Typically located in suburban areas, HLM complexes are supervised by public authorities with the aim of ensuring access to housing for a wide range of socio-economic groups, although they are often associated with low-income populations with precarious legal status in French society.

I started my life in this HLM because it was impossible for me to find accommodation when I applied to French universities while in China, and hence I had to use a study abroad agent (not a common service in the early 2000s) to help me find any possible accommodation when I arrived in France. I later learnt that as a foreign student without institutional ties or relatives to provide guarantor documents, it was almost impossible to find accommodation from China. This systemic barrier – rooted in a society where access to resources often depends on social status and cultural background – was a shared reality for many Asian, African, and South American students navigating France independently as well as for French citizens of immigrant descent with humble economic and social resources.

My first neighbourhood in France was made up of often stigmatised and largely neglected groups, including a variety of immigrants, asylum seekers, and marginalised groups from former French colonies and elsewhere. My apartment complex was a melting pot of nationalities, races, and cultures, but there was a notable absence of white French people in this otherwise diverse environment. These were people who, like me, had been stripped of 'labels' they had acquired in the previous social environments where they lived. I met people from the Central and East Asia, Africa, Eastern Europe – many with complex, precarious legal statuses – trying to make ends meet in a society that barely recognised their existence. I could not help but notice the glaring contradictions between the values of equality and freedom so loudly proclaimed in French official discourse and narratives, and the lived realities of the people I met. It was here that I first encountered the reality of European racial and social hierarchies and colonial legacies.

In the following years, during my time as a foreign student in Lyon, I continued to encounter the harsh realities of life that often lie beneath the surface of academic pursuits. France is country known for its high cost of living; this was particularly challenging for someone from an ordinary urban Chinese family. Therefore, to support myself financially, I took on a variety of part-time jobs during my extended student years – these ranged from babysitting, housecleaning, ironing, caring for the disabled, private language teacher, translator, tourist guide, to university teaching assistant.

In France, it is common for students to take on small jobs to help bridge the gap between their studies and the cost of living. My experiences in these roles did not distinguish me as a foreigner; rather, they allowed me to connect with a diverse group of marginalised individuals, many of whom shared similar socio-economic struggles. A common thread emerged between us: we were all experiencing financial anxiety and insecurity, often struggling to live what many would consider a decent or comfortable life; many of us were from 'other countries', and a majority of us were females.

These experiences reinforced my earlier observations about the covert segregation that permeates French society, rooted in race, ethnicity, national origin, and social backgrounds. But I also became increasingly aware of how power dynamics privilege not only the 'middle class, white, French citizens', but also the wealthy, educated, and predominantly male members of society, positioning them at the centre while relegating others to the periphery. And to perceive these power dynamics and hierarchical structures behind the 'multicultural, equal' surface that the official French narratives and many academic works have successfully established around the world, one has to put oneself in the middle of real life, breathing, working, speaking, and living the realities of as many people as possible, in as many layers of society as possible. To sum up, my time in Lyon reinforced my belief in the need to immerse oneself in real-life experiences to understand the complexity of social hierarchies.

Story 1. First encounter: Panic on the margins of French society

It was a first 'cultural shock' to arrive at the HLM complex on the outskirts of Lyon. As our car pulled in, a group of children – none of whom looked like the 'blonde, blue-eyed French kids' I'd imagined – threw small stones at us. These were the children of immigrant families, many from France's former colonies in North and West Africa, and their brown and black faces reflected the racialised poverty and systemic neglect that characterise these neighbourhoods. For families like theirs, the HLM blocks were both a lifeline and a trap: spaces of concentrated marginalisation to which non-white, working-class immigrants were often relegated.

This was my first direct encounter with France's unspoken hierarchies – a stark counterpoint to the myth of 'equality, liberty, and fraternity' I'd absorbed through books and the media. The ideals I'd associated with Europe dissolved into the reality of postcolonial inequality, where opportunity depended not only on class but also on race and origin.

Just two weeks after moving into the housing complex, my bag was stolen when I left my room to wash dishes in the communal kitchen down the hall. My wallet, a camera, and my passport were in the bag (I had to take it with me every day as I was looking for new accommodations, and most estate agents required an original passport). It was a terrifying experience: this was before the age of smartphones and social media; I had to use a pre-paid international phone card and go down to the phone booth to call my parents in China. Although I had studied French for two years in my spare time, it was still a huge challenge to understand and express myself fluently during my first six months in France. At that time, I could barely speak a sentence or two in French without searching for words, and I had no close friends or anyone to call for help. Losing my passport was like losing my whole identity that I had brought with me from China, as though my whole life was tied up in that identity document!

I still remember the panic, fear, and helplessness I felt that night. Luckily there was a girl from Kunming in the same group of new arrivals who accompanied me and comforted me, which was such a blessing at the time. It was also the first time I realised that when you are stripped of all the protections and advantages that come with social labels (cultural identities, titles, degrees, family background, social and financial status), you are in 'survival mode', and the sense of 'belonging' will be no longer based on shared passions for music or films, values, or views (these become the criteria for the 'next level'), but on basic sympathy and lived, shared human experiences.

The next morning, we went early to the local lost property office. Miraculously, someone had found my bag in a nearby bin and returned it – with my passport still inside. Beyond immense gratitude for this unexpected kindness, the experience left me with a deeper reflection. In that moment of helplessness, I felt the power of trust – trust in the unknown, in unseen care, and in life's unexpected blessings. Yet, beneath this relief lay a harsher truth: the theft was not just an unfortunate incident but a symptom of deeper systemic neglect. In marginalised neighborhoods, where precariousness and lack of regulation prevail, desperation takes root. These communities, excluded from France's universalist ideals, are often left to fend for themselves, caught in cycles that perpetuate insecurity and survival-driven acts.

Although I stayed for only two months, the HLM changed my understanding of France. My tiny room – a luxury after sharing a dormitory in China – was surrounded by a melting pot of nationalities: an Algerian girl working three shifts, a Central African family battling bureaucracy over legal paperwork, a Polish cleaner who'd once taught literature. Their struggles reflected my own invisibility in a society that preached 'equality and fraternity' but reduced us to labels: immigrant, foreign student, 'black worker', other.

Here, the promise of 'equality' gave way to hierarchies shaped by race and class. The near-total absence of white French residents in this supposedly 'diverse' neighbourhood highlighted the segregation woven into France's social fabric. These suburbs, omitted from the glossy narratives of official institutions, revealed the contradictions of Enlightenment universalism – a framework that, far from rewarding merit alone, was deeply intertwined with historical power structures favouring whiteness and colonial legacies.

In the periphery of Lyon, I had entered the wider narrative of being 'othered', and for the first time I began to fully comprehend the weight and the materiality of the term Eurocentrism, which gradually replaced my idealistic notion of an 'Enlightened Europe' as the leading model of humane societies that I had previously believed in. This was the 'other' France, where Eurocentrism was masquerading as progress. My ideal of an 'enlightened Europe' crumbled, replaced by the visceral reality of post-colonial inequality.

The HLM also humbled me, stripping me of privileges I'd taken for granted in China: the security of belonging, the currency of academic titles. Survival here demanded solidarity forged not in shared ideals but in shared vulnerability. This revelation – that systemic structures, not individual merit, determine who thrives – anchored my research. The Enlightenment's 'universal' ideals, I realised, were never universal at all. They served only those deemed worthy by race, class, gender, or colonial origin.

Story 2. The limits of comparison: Navigating Eurocentrism through the academic landscape

As I prepared to embark on my academic journey in France, I was confident and excited; my BA thesis was a first comparative study of absurdity in the works of contemporary Chinese writer Wang Xiaobo and Albert Camus. My supervisor at Peking University, a professor of Comparative Literature with a focus on French Literature, graded my work with merit and provided supportive comments that reinforced my belief in the value of cross-cultural literary exploration. I saw my time in France as a precious opportunity to delve deeper into the two literary traditions, especially with a direct and authentic experience of French literature, which I had only studied through translated works and Chinese intellectual commentaries.

I vividly recall my first meeting with Professor Gregory Lee, then head of Chinese Studies at Université Jean-Moulin Lyon 3. Professor Lee is a prominent scholar whose research includes Chinese studies, transcultural studies, and post-colonial theory. A focus of his work is the intersection of Chinese culture and post-colonial theory, analysing how Chinese modernity is shaped by colonial histories and global transformations. He also founded the Transcultural and Transtextual Institute, where I carried out my PhD project later. This institute is a unique research centre that includes students from different social and cultural backgrounds, including those traditionally 'marginalised' in the traditionally European-dominated academic world in France, such as Vietnam, Brazil, Ukraine, and Taiwan.

I remember sitting in Professor Lee's office, an underground room in the university library. The room was simple and small, with no windows, but lined with shelves full of books on Chinese poetry, literature, culture, and philosophy. In the same underground space, there were also references to 'other areas' such as Middle Eastern and Russian literature. Excitement coursed through me as I shared my desire and vision to further explore the vast literary landscapes beyond through the comparative works of the authors from China and France. However, my enthusiasm was met with a disheartening revelation: Professor Lee informed me, with a somewhat bitter smile: 'Well, Chinese literature does not fall within the scope of comparative literature here, at least not yet.'

This moment struck me as profoundly revelatory, challenging the very ideals of 'universality' that many European official discourses and scholarly works proudly claim to uphold. Here I was, at the heart of a nation celebrated for its Enlightenment values and intellectual traditions, only to find my literary roots relegated to a peripheral category alongside those of 'other' East Asian or 'Oriental cultures'. It was at this moment that I began to grasp the profound meaning of 'Orientalism' as articulated by Edward Said three decades earlier. The imperialist power structures that shape how Eastern cultures are understood and represented in the West became glaringly apparent to me – this time not just as an abstract concept, but as an embodied, personal experience.

While I had prepared myself to navigate the complexities of reading and writing in French, I learnt that, as of 2006, Chinese literature was largely excluded from the field of Comparative Literature in most French institutions. Unlike conventional Western literatures that dominate the curriculum, Chinese literature occupied only a niche role. It was typically taught alongside Chinese language courses under the broader umbrella of foreign languages and civilisations. For students specifically interested in Chinese literature, the subject was often subsumed under Asian or Oriental Studies. Only a few elite institutions – such as the École Normale Supérieure (ENS) and INALCO (Institut National des Langues et Civilisations Orientales) – offered specialised programmes that might include contemporary Chinese writers in a Comparative Literature framework. For instance, INALCO was presented as a prestigious centre dedicated to the teaching and research of non-European languages and civilisations, colloquially known as 'Langues O' (short for Langues Orientales), which encompasses more than 100 languages from around the world, with a particular focus on Asia, Africa, Eastern Europe, the Middle East, and Oceania.

I suddenly realised that the acronym 'O' here stood not only for a geographical 'oriental' area but also for a structural and institutional 'otherness'; the 'O' distinguishes all the 'others' that are not identified as 'Western Europe' and puts them all in an isolated, somehow 'exotic' box – a prestigious academic institute that focuses only on them. While Chinese universities also have categories such as 'French Studies', 'Hispanic Studies', or 'Middle East Studies', these were still part of the same university unit and occupied a parallel place as 'Chinese Studies' departments. The sense of hierarchy or the distinction between 'central' and 'peripheral' in terms of academic disciplines was less obvious in China, at least on the surface.

Years later, when I started working as an academic member at a British university, I realised that this is the same model as the famous institute SOAS (School of Oriental and African Studies) in London, specialising in the study of Asia, Africa, and the Middle East. The 'segregation' actually happens not only beyond the socio-political boundaries but also in the middle of the production, categorisation, and dissemination of knowledge.

This realisation forced me to reconsider the term 'World Literature'. What I had assumed to signify 'all literary traditions globally' instead appeared, in the French academic context of the early 2000s, to denote a far narrower scope – one largely confined to Western Europe. Regions like Asia, along with so-called Oriental territories, remained peripheral in this framework. This awareness illuminated the contours of a power dynamic that extended beyond the social fabric of France that I had begun to observe and experience from the HLM complex, and penetrated to the very heart of how knowledge is classified, validated, and valued, from the 'centre' of knowledge – just as the myth of rock.

My recognition of these entrenched power dynamics and hierarchies within the academic field in France also became one of the major motivations for me to choose to interrogate Chinese rock (*Yaogun*) as my PhD project. I began to see that my perception of rock music – and specifically Chinese rock – was strikingly like the way I perceived Chinese literature. Under the influence of the myths of an 'Enlightened Europe' or a 'Revolution for Freedom', I had imagined rock music to be a universal form of resistance, an expression that transcended cultural and geographic boundaries. Just as I thought I shared the same ideals of 'literature' across cultures, I believed that rock would be a common ground of defiance, a bridge across differences. However, the bitter reality I faced in France was that almost nobody had ever heard of Chinese rock music, and many didn't even know it existed, even though rock music had been developing in China since Cui Jian for about three decades.

The stark contrast between my idealisation and the reality I faced in both literature and music highlighted the gap between my personal imagination and the reality shaped by 'the centre of knowledge and liberal values'. It was this realisation that drove me to examine Chinese rock, not just as a musical genre, but as a cultural and socio-political phenomenon, deserving of exploration and recognition within global discourses.

In the end, going to France was as much about escaping as it was about seeking the expectations that had defined me in China while seeking a different way of understanding myself and my place in the world. The experience stripped away my naive romanticism and replaced it with a more grounded understanding of what true freedom and equality might look like. It set the stage for a deeper, more nuanced exploration of my identity – one that embraced the complexities and contradictions of both my heritage and my aspirations. And though the myth of an 'enlightened Europe' may have faded, the journey it inspired was far from over; it led me to understand that the quest for enlightenment is not tied to a particular country but is instead an ongoing, internal process – a realisation that also guided me to turn back to Chinese and other Eastern classical philosophies, like Daoism and Buddhism, which became my personal spiritual path during my years in France.

Looking back, it was an ironic path: when I was living in China, I was fascinated by rock music and all the Western cultures and values about 'individual voice, freedom, rebellion spirit'. But it was only when I left China and lived in the West that I rediscovered the profound wisdom in Daoism and Buddhism, such as 'non-attachment to ego, selflessness, emptiness, and the interdependence of the human, the law of nature, and the environment' from my Eastern heritage, my own cultural roots. It seems that we might need to leave to 'find', and we might be able to better get to know ourselves through contact and exchange with 'others'.

My journey interrogating Chinese rock and social change seemed complete when I finally finished my PhD in France in 2014, but my personal journey of self-discovery, of 'deconstruction and reconstruction' around the sense of 'who I am' and 'where I belong' was not. As I left France to take up a position at a British university, my next chapter was about to begin in a not-so-distant but still very different setting – one that had been one of the most important empires of the nineteenth century: the British Empire. Not only was it one of the most important empires in modern human history, but it was also the centre of the Industrial Revolution and the place where Karl Marx wrote his famous works on capitalism. This new social context carried its own weight of history, contradictions, and legacies. While I was ready to continue my journey of self-exploration within its intricate socio-cultural tapestry, I didn't know what kind of new discoveries or new disillusionments lay ahead and what kind of realisation would unfold along this seemingly never-ending path.

8
Departing France for England: The third move and the disillusionment with the 'liberal world'

Leaving China for France was, for me, a significant leap into an idealised, imagined 'Enlightened Europe'. This move began a long process of disillusionment. A gradual unravelling of my idealised notions of the West, as represented by France, and of much of a big part of my self-perception, constructed with this idealised notion. Leaving France for the United Kingdom, by comparison, felt less drastic – both practically and emotionally. After a decade in France, navigating its complexities and contradictions and undergoing the 'deconstruction and reconstruction' of my sense of identity, I felt more prepared for what awaited me in England. Yet this move marked another crucial shift in my cross-cultural experience, filled with both anticipation and the undertones of new disillusionments.

My familiarity with the English language dates to my schooling in China, where English was the first foreign language I learnt – long before I started learning French. From the mid-1980s, every Chinese student who completed the 'Nine-Year Compulsory Education'[21] had some foundation in English, both as a language and as a cultural entity. In the 1990s, Longman, a well-known British publisher, worked with Chinese education authorities to produce English textbooks as part of a wider effort to improve English language skills at a time of China's increasing openness to the global world and market. These textbooks, co-published with the People's Education Press (PEP), were used nationwide in the 1990s, and I was among those whose English learning journey began with these books. For many of the 'post-80s' generation, including myself, these textbooks are unforgettable, filled with main Chinese characters like Li Lei, Han Meimei, and their English friends, namely James Green, who had a pet parrot called Polly, and his sister Kate, who had a black cat. These characters were, in a way, our first symbolic link to the wider English-speaking world beyond China.

As we moved into the twenty-first century, Hollywood movies and American popular culture, especially popular music, became increasingly influential in mainland China, drawing us towards another more 'updated' and 'fresher' version of the English-speaking world. For me, however, England held an additional sense of familiarity beyond the language lessons. A big part of the rock music icons and legendary bands that I had heard of and listened to – bands like the Beatles, the Rolling Stones, Pink Floyd, and the raw energy of punk – came from this cultural sphere, yet I had never really lived in an English-speaking world since graduating from university and leaving China. In my imaginary world, England was not just a place; it held a deep cultural resonance for me, a sense of continuity constructed by the myth of rock music and the subsequent 'product' – my PhD project on rock in China, which I incidentally carried out in a 'not so rock' country like France. So as I prepared for my new chapter in life in England, I hoped it would provide some comfort amid the uncertainties of a new move.

A decade earlier, I was a naive, young 'elite' Chinese student who loved rock music; I thought I was 'authentic and cool'. But coming from China with no 'recognised' credentials and labels related to my social identity in a totally different social and cultural context, I immediately realised that I was a 'nobody' in a world with a completely different system of evaluation and standards. By the time I moved to the United Kingdom, I had done my master's and PhD in French universities and had somehow acquired some intercultural knowledge and experience. Meanwhile, the world has changed a great deal between the mid-2000s and the time I wrote this book. The most significant changes have been in technology. The social media (Facebook, Twitter, YouTube) were all born in the mid-2000s, and in 2007, Steve Jobs announced the launch of the first iPhone – the most famous smart mobile device that would fundamentally change the way people communicate and relate to each other.

By 2016, the year I moved to the United Kingdom, I no longer needed to buy a physical phone card in the Asian supermarket and use a public phone booth to call my family. I could now reach them anytime through my smartphone, via Skype, Facetime, WeChat, and so on. I also had a job offer from an English university, which in many ways guarantees a lot of 'recognised' social credits and facilities on my personal profile when navigating essential tasks for all people immigrating from one country to another, such as having a legal residence status, finding accommodation, opening a bank account, and the like.

In this context, moving to England seemed like a smoother transition compared to my arrival in France a decade earlier. The United Kingdom was still part of the European Union when I moved – ironically, I arrived just as Brexit happened, complicating the country's position within Western Europe almost overnight. I was prepared for similar bureaucratic struggles – finding accommodation, dealing with banks, and navigating the administrative processes for legal paperwork as a foreign citizen – a bureaucratic nightmare for many 'foreigners' living in France; but surprisingly everything seemed easier.

Within two weeks of arriving in Liverpool, I had found a decent place to live. Finding a stable home in France took me two long years of paperwork and setbacks, but in Liverpool, it all came down to my job offer and proof of income – making the process much simpler and smoother. My first impression of Liverpool was positive and hopeful; the demographic landscape in Liverpool was quite diverse: people speaking different languages or English with different accents, coming from different cultural, social, and religious backgrounds, with a wide range of racial and ethnic features, seemingly occupying relatively parallel spaces in public places. There seemed to be no clearly visible 'dominant mainstream (white European) group' in most social settings, at least on the surface. I thought to myself, perhaps this 'liberal world' I was entering wouldn't frustrate me with the same stark, invisible barriers as it had in France a decade earlier.

But living and working in Liverpool soon led to a new phase of disillusionment. Liverpool's rich history – as a port city shaped by colonialism, the slave trade, and waves of immigration – was evident in its enduring social orders. Beneath its outwardly cosmopolitan façade, the city still maintained layers of a capitalist 'liberal world' that promised intercultural diversity, inclusivity, equality, and available opportunity. These promises, integral to the concept of neoliberalism – a system characterised by deregulation, privatisation, and market-driven growth (Harvey, 2005) – and digital cosmopolitanism – the idea that digital connectivity promotes global inclusivity (Castells, 2010) – began to unravel on closer inspection.

On a personal level, the decision to leave France for the United Kingdom felt like a return to the initial uncertainty I had experienced when I first left China. Once again, it was a leap into the unknown. This time, however, the weight of the journey carried far more complexity, both for myself and for my mother. It wasn't simply about moving to another country or chasing an education; it was about facing the expectations that had begun to loom larger as I approached the symbolic age of 30. In the eyes of my family – and Chinese society at large – I was no longer just a young student in her early twenties setting out on a journey of discovery. I was now a woman who had spent more than 25 of my 30 years of life immersed in education, who had finally completed a PhD in Europe, but who was still not ready to 'go back to my roots' and 'settle down'. Instead, I wanted to start a new chapter in another country, with a different language, culture, and with zero social connections – even further away from my parents.

When I informed my mother of my intention to move, after I passed the interview and got the job offer from the University of Liverpool, I could see the concern carved more deeply into her face. I knew this time it wasn't the same kind of worry she had when I first left China. In fact, when I moved to France, she embraced the idea despite her reservations. But even she, in all her progressive attitudes, had limits shaped by an upbringing steeped in Confucian values, social expectations, and the lingering legacy of patriarchal norms. Though she never said it directly, I could sense the underlying message in her expressions and tone: 'You have already defied social norms by leaving China and pursuing a PhD in France, spending a decade far from family as a girl and a single child. Now that you've achieved this, it's time to return to your roots, support your aging parents, and settle down with your own family. Especially as a Chinese woman at your age, you're approaching the boundary of what society deems acceptable.'

When I finished my PhD in 2014, I had reached a significant milestone in my life. I had studied for more than two decades and had just turned 30. For my parents, family, and peers, this meant that I had to think about establishing myself in a different way. There is an old saying in Chinese culture, 三十而立 ('Establish yourself at the age of thirty') – a famous quote by Confucius that every Chinese knows by heart because it is included in school textbooks as part of classical literary education. It emphasises stability, finding one's place in the world, and building a home.

The expectation for women was even more precise: marry by 25, have children by 30, start a family – become a nurturing cornerstone of society. For my mother, the sight of me leaving France to go to the United Kingdom, seemingly unanchored and with no desire to start a family of my own, was deeply unsettling. She feared I would become a 'wild, single woman with a PhD', wandering the world alone with no place to call home.

Moving from France to the United Kingdom was not easy for me. After ten years in France, I had built a life, accumulated some resources, and learnt to navigate the rules and cultural codes of a society that at first felt completely foreign. I had struggled, but I had also found my place. I had a partner at the time, but it was not the kind of relationship where I felt called to settle down. In a way, I had begun to appreciate the comfort of familiarity – the way I knew how to approach a shopkeeper or strike up a conversation with a stranger in a café. Nevertheless, I decided to leave it all behind once again, drawn by an inexplicable sense of unfinished exploration, fuelled by a boundless curiosity about the world, its diverse cultures and people. I wanted to continue exploring, not only the outside world, but also to discover more about myself through these encounters with 'others'.

To my mother, I suppose, this move seemed like a rejection of the very ideals she had hoped I would eventually embrace. She always made it clear that she was proud of me, but during the years of my PhD, both my parents' reminders about finding a partner and starting a family became more frequent and pointed. I knew it wasn't just my parents' voices – it was the voice of Chinese society and many other Asian societies that still held prejudices against women who remained single after a certain age (with 30 being a significant symbolic milestone), especially those with advanced academic qualifications. This sentiment was deeply ingrained and echoed by countless others, forming a cultural backdrop that made the pressure all the more tangible. All my Chinese female friends who had followed similar paths or prioritised their professional or personal pursuits over starting a family shared the same story and felt the same pressure. The Chinese term '大龄剩女' ('leftover woman') loomed over me, frequently used by my father as a joke to mock my personal status – a persistent reminder that I was deviating from an unspoken social contract. Jokes about female PhD holders being 'the third type of human' ('the third sex') were never out of earshot in Chinese society, casually thrown around to undermine the ambitions of women like me, who dared to prioritise intellectual pursuits over societal expectations.

And so, when I chose to move to the United Kingdom, my mother was conflicted. She appreciated my independence and determination, just as she had once been determined to chart her own path as a young woman. Yet, her unease was evident. She worried about me starting over again, with no personal connections or support system. She worried about the uncertain future of her daughter who had become, in her eyes, a scholar without a home – someone whose journey seemed endless, whose destination remained elusive.

This tension became a recurring theme in our conversations – a quiet undercurrent woven into my research on rock music and cultural identity. My academic focus on rock music and societal transformation, particularly within systems shaped by norms and power dynamics, began to mirror my personal journey: a struggle against the roles assigned to me as a woman and a daughter by the Chinese society. My mother never ceased to be proud of me, but her pride was always tinged with a growing anxiety – an anxiety that seemed to deepen with each new degree, each achievement, and each further step away from home. So perhaps the greatest challenge for me in all these moves over the years hasn't been facing the unknown alone, but dealing with the unspoken disapproval of those closest to me – parents, relatives, childhood friends, and the society that was supposed to be my 'motherland' at large – who felt increasingly distanced from the path I had chosen. They could not really understand why pursuits like 'finding a home' or 'settling down', which seemed so fundamental to them, were not priorities for me. In the quiet moments of our conversations, there was always the echo of a series of unspoken questions: Why can't you just be happy with a 'normal life'? What are you ultimately looking for? When will you finally arrive? And arrive at what?

As I reflect on the present, I often think about how, from a Buddhist perspective, I am deeply karmically connected to the United Kingdom and to Liverpool. Not only was it the city where I began my academic journey as a scholar after many years of study; it also happened to be the place where my supervisor, Professor Lee, was born and raised; it was also a city to which I'd been drawn years earlier, albeit in a more complex and disappointing way. This connection began in 2009, when I attempted to visit Liverpool as part of my doctoral research – a journey that ended with a visa refusal, an experience that profoundly reshaped my understanding of the limits of freedom and the barriers to global mobility.

A pre-history of my life in the United Kingdom: Visa rejection and the collision with the limits of freedom

By 2009, I had earned two master's degrees in France: one in Chinese Studies and another in French as a Foreign Language, both from public universities in Lyon. These choices emerged from the collapse of my original plan to pursue Comparative Literature.

The Chinese Studies programme felt natural – as a native speaker with a BA in Chinese language and literature, I already had deep roots in the subject. Yet it also reshaped my understanding of modern China. For the first time, I engaged critically with the May Fourth Movement of 1919, not merely as a historical footnote in Chinese modern history but as a multifaceted phenomenon: a youth-led protest demanding radical social change, a symbolic rupture with tradition, and a lens exposing global power hierarchies. This time, it was no longer abstract theory; it echoed my own lived experiences in France.

The programme also introduced me to the overlooked histories of Chinese diaspora communities in Europe. Through this, I met Professor Gregory Lee, my future PhD supervisor, and discovered his Transcultural and Transtextual Institute – a space where borders between cultures and texts dissolved.

This time, my project was bold – even unorthodox in the French academic context: an exploration of Chinese rock music. The first year of my PhD involved navigating scarce academic literature on the topic, scouring media archives, and piecing together fragments from the internet. As a self-funded student, I balanced three part-time jobs throughout my PhD to stay afloat.

During my second year, an opportunity arose to expand my research. With support from Professor Lee and a host professor at Liverpool Hope University, I secured a regional grant promoting international academic exchange. After a gruelling application process, I received €3,600 in funding and a six-month stipend for a research stay in Liverpool. For someone juggling multiple jobs, this wasn't just financial relief – it was a gateway to a city steeped in musical legend. Liverpool, birthplace of the Beatles and a symbol of rock's rebellious spirit, felt like a promised land.

As someone raised on the myths of rock – stories of John Lennon singing 'Imagine all the people, living life in peace', 'All we are saying is give peace a chance' from a hotel bed; Pink Floyd's epic cry of 'Hey, teacher, leave them kids alone!' in *Another Brick in the Wall*; and the Queen's roar of 'We Will Rock You' – Britain seemed like the cradle, the ultimate pantheon of rock. For me and countless others of my generation in China, who had absorbed the dreams and despair of the Western rock scenes through the myth built up by words in magazines, snippets of songs and videos on TV and radio, and of the 1960s and 1970s through books, translated biographies, and rare tapes, this was more than a field trip – it was almost a pilgrimage.

But the cold reality soon crept in. As a Chinese passport holder, I needed a visa to enter the United Kingdom. My scholarship – approved, endorsed, and sponsored by the French Ministry of Education – wasn't enough to get me through the tedious bureaucracy that would follow. After studying the visa categories on the website of the British Home Office, I applied for an 'Academic Visitor Visa', the only visa category suitable for my six-month stay, without thinking twice. I was sure that I would get my visa without any problems – I had applied for a 'Visitor Visa' as a tourist some years ago and got it. This time, armed with a regional government grant and the invitation letter from the British host university, it seemed that my profile only looked better with more 'official endorsement'. I eagerly began preparations: finding someone to sublet my room in Lyon, organising my research materials, even mentally mapping out which record stores and music venues I would visit in Liverpool.

Then came the rejection.

A cold letter with no clear explanation. My passport returned with a simple stamp saying 'UK PARIS', a line crossed over it – an empty gesture, signifying the closure of possibilities. I remember holding my passport and staring at the stark insignia for what felt like hours. What did it mean to be denied entry? What was I being denied beyond a visa? Perhaps the ability to imagine the world as open, as belonging equally to those willing to explore it. Perhaps the right to believe that there was a 'liberal world' out there that welcomed difference. This silent refusal from the British consulate marked the end of what I had imagined would be a chapter of exploration and excitement. Instead, it became a moment of disillusionment – one that reminded me of my limitations, of the boundaries set not by my own curiosity but by a larger, indifferent system, very much influenced by the wider geopolitical environment and vested interests far beyond my personal reach and understanding at the time.

I remember the frustration and the sense of helplessness that followed. Here I was, with a scholarship that should have symbolised international academic exchange, blocked by a simple and arbitrary bureaucratic decision. I tried to appeal the rejection, but the British Embassy in Paris seems such a high, distant, solid bureaucratic entity, representing a once dominant imperialist country, that it was impossible to reach for someone like me – a foreign doctoral student of Asian background, and an individual who had to apply for a visa because her identity document was tied to an ideological entity that had a contradictory and complex relationship with Britain, and perhaps with the whole 'liberal world'. In the end, despite repeated attempts to contact both regional scholarship administrators and officials at the British Embassy, endless robotic, distant responses, I was left without any concrete answers. I had gradually come to a realisation: This wasn't just a visa refusal; it was a stark reminder of my place in the global order.

In fact, it turned out that I was the first Chinese recipient – and first rejection – of that regional grant. Previous awardees, all from EU nations, moved freely in an era of assumed mobility. My status as a non-European outlier, straddling French and British bureaucracies, revealed the unspoken terms of 'open' systems: access hinged on predetermined scripts of belonging.

There was a bitter note at the end of that chapter, and I let go of the opportunity. In the end, I didn't get the grant either – the terms of the scholarship stipulated that I had to be physically present in Liverpool to receive the funding, and without a visa this was impossible. After a few anxious nights of poor sleep and a long internal process of questioning, I informed the scholarship committee and my supervisor of my decision to voluntarily give up the scholarship, and so my dream of visiting Liverpool slipped away.

Strangely, letting go brought unexpected clarity. The experience reframed my understanding of agency: not resistance, but detachment. I came to a deep understanding of lines from the Buddhist scripture *Heart Sutra* (心经): '心无挂碍，无挂碍故无有恐怖', ('when the mind is free from attachments, clinging, or obstacles, it can experience true freedom, and as a result, fear also ceases to exist'). The Taoist proverb 福祸相依 (interdependence of fortune/misfortune) also shifted from abstract concepts to lived truths. These philosophies, long embedded in my cultural roots, now resonated as fluid frameworks for navigating rigid 'fate'. In a way, the disappointing visa rejection and my 'giving up' symbolically ignited the seed of longing for 'ultimate freedom' and a fundamental 'equanimity' in my inner world.

The rejection also exposed the myth of seamless globalisation. The 'flat world' narrative (Friedman, 2005), promoted by those unconstrained by borders and other socio-political regimes, dissolved into paradox. Years later, at the University of Liverpool, an email arrived: the French scholarship office sought advice for an African applicant who was similarly denied entry. When I read that email, I felt a strange mix of emotions – vindication, sadness, and an unavoidable sense of irony – the irony echoed Camus' absurdism – a theme I'd once aimed to explore academically. I had also come to realise a bitter fact: although I had moved on from that particular episode, the shadow of exclusion remained and was repeated in the experiences of others like me; the so-called liberal world wasn't built for everyone. Distinction and exclusion, it seemed, repeated itself cyclically, but now under another shiny label of 'digital cosmopolitanism', seamlessly integrated into the perspective and logic of neoliberalism.

On the surface, my visa refusal seemed to suggest that passports – not potential – dictate life trajectories. But deeper reflection revealed a broader structural irony: the myth of neoliberalism, sold through seductive narratives of 'globalisation' and 'free movement', paradoxically entrenches the very inequalities it claims to resolve. Neoliberalism's ideological scaffolding, rooted in market fundamentalism, frames privatisation, deregulation, and hyper-individualism as moral imperatives (Harvey, 2005). By casting individuals as entrepreneurial agents solely responsible for their fate, it naturalises exclusion – whether through border regimes that stratify mobility or digital economies that masquerade as democratising forces (Ong, 2006). What emerges is a world in which the rhetoric of opportunity obscures systemic hierarchies: elites navigate borders and algorithms with ease, while marginalised populations face exclusion coded as personal failure (Brown, 2015).

Moreover, global digital and technology giants such as Amazon, Twitter, and Uber, once hailed as facilitators of economic democracy, now function as monopolistic enterprises that consolidate wealth and power in the hands of a few, replicating and reinforcing the very exclusions they claimed to dismantle. Yanis Varoufakis (2023) critiques this phenomenon as *digital feudalism*, arguing that these platforms no longer operate as traditional free markets but as centralised fiefdoms where users and workers are subjected to algorithmic control, surveillance, and exploitation without democratic oversight. This digital landscape, rather than flattening borders or democratising opportunity, erects new frontiers of exclusion – ones dictated not by geography but by platform capitalism's capacity to extract value while maintaining strict control over participation (Varoufakis, 2023). The rejection of visas, then, is not merely a bureaucratic inconvenience but a symptom of a broader ideological structure that commodifies human mobility, restricting access to the so-called liberal world to those deemed economically and socially viable.

Navigating neoliberal logic in the British academic system

My academic journey began in the School of Humanities at the University of Liverpool, an interdisciplinary space dedicated to languages, cultures, and social systems. At a time when global academia was increasingly prioritising STEM fields, the humanities offered a counterpoint – a space where ambiguity and systemic critique were not only tolerated but valued. But even here, the intrusion of neoliberal logic was inevitable. British academia, like much of the higher education landscape in the global North, has been reshaped by market-driven imperatives that privilege economic utility over critical inquiry. Funding allocations have disproportionately favoured STEM disciplines, while institutional performance has been quantified through mechanisms such as the Research Excellence Framework (REF) – a system that ostensibly ensures quality but often replicates corporate metrics of productivity and commodified knowledge. This shift reflects what Stephen Ball (2012) calls the 'neoliberalisation' of education: the subordination of intellectual inquiry to market efficiency, where students and scholars alike are recast as 'entrepreneurial subjects' in a transactional system. Humanities programmes, with their resistance to quantifiable outcomes, increasingly function as relics in an academy that rewards compliance with neoliberal norms – norms that mirror the broader social hierarchies I had encountered on the border years earlier.

Turning education into a business: A system that maintains and reinforces social hierarchies

Before I came to the United Kingdom to take up an academic position in a public research university, I imagined myself surrounded by colleagues, engaged in deep discussions and exchanges about our research topics, sharing the questions on our minds, working together to find answers or constructive solutions to the challenges we face in society, just as I'd been doing during my PhD journey in France. But it didn't take long for me to feel that something was fundamentally different. I began to realise that the university environment in the United Kingdom was structured less around intellectual exchange and more around the careful balancing of budgets, metrics, and market positioning. I often felt that I had joined a corporation rather than an academic institution.

My early days in the British university were a period of adjustment, filled with dissonant experiences. Many meetings were driven by conversations around spreadsheets of performance indicators, the latest National Student Survey results, and how we could tweak our methods to improve these figures. The focus was on keeping our 'customers' – our students – happy to protect and enhance our part of the institution. Having pursued a self-funded doctorate at a French public university, where tuition was minimal and bureaucracy was rigid yet far from the corporate ethos of British academia, this language felt foreign: recruitment figures, impact metrics, satisfaction scales – it all echoed a business model. I often sat in a daze, realising how little space remained for the academic reflection that had drawn me to this field in the first place.

The neoliberal perspective has become increasingly invasive in recent years, effectively turning everyone involved in this metric into players in a game that benefits only a small elite group, just like the whole social structure it represents. I can't count the number of times I've had to shelve a promising research or project idea or put aside a long-awaited reading for 'later', only to have that 'later' swallowed up by yet another meeting or metrics-related task. In this framework, there is no room for failure or 'inefficiency', no patience for ideas that need time to percolate, and certainly no tolerance for projects that don't fit into the pre-defined boxes of impact with measurable outcomes (better presented in the form of statistics and shiny graphs). All this reminds me of my earlier days in China as a teenager, as a 'model student', a 'good daughter', and a 'nice girl', and I had to navigate these roles with perfect alignment, there was no room for doubt, failure, or withdrawal, as a girl there's even no room for 'anger'.

In the end, it seems that what rock music had awakened in my inner world, allowing me to step out of my 'comfort zone' and be 'authentic', took me a long way across France and put me 'back in the same box' in the United Kingdom. I found myself imprisoned again – this time by a system cloaked in the rhetoric of an 'open, fair, inclusive' world. The 'same box', I realised, was not geographical but ideological: a global commodification of culture and knowledge, enforced by a pragmatic and meritocratic ethos that prioritises material gain and social capital over personal growth, well-being, and critical inquiry. Whether in China's rigid social roles, France's bureaucracy, or Britain's cooperative academia, the same pattern emerged: institutions reward conformity to narrow values while marginalising dissent.

I often wonder what we're really creating here. When I talk to students, many of them are under immense pressure to pass the module with a 'first grade', which would guarantee 'first-class student' status on their CV, so that they can eventually apply for a better-placed, better-paid job in an increasingly competitive job market, with more and more limited opportunities that aren't really 'open to all', especially in certain fields that have traditionally been dominated by an elite, closed group of people. The whole circle reminds me of the familiar setting of the Chinese *gaokao* – the fiercely competitive entrance exam for higher education – with a familiar logic of 'good grades lead to good jobs and social status, which equals a good life'. It is a beautiful promise that only highlights the potential rewards without mentioning the high personal costs it may entail – a beautiful promise that puts immense pressure on every high school student and their parents.

Framed as a beacon of 'global opportunity', the UK higher education system reinforces entrenched hierarchies through its financial architecture. International students – disproportionately from the global South – face tuition fees three times higher than their domestic counterparts, a disparity that reflects wider global inequalities. For many families in regions such as rural China or

Eastern Europe, even 'affordable' UK degrees remain astronomically out of reach, locked behind paywalls that conflate access with privilege.

There is a paradox in this system: it markets itself as meritocratic while structurally excluding those without generational wealth. Elite institutions such as Oxford exemplify this, and here admissions criteria – honed by extracurricular coaching and linguistic fluency – favour applicants who can afford years of preparatory investment. For most in the global South, such benchmarks seem insurmountable, not for lack of ambition, but because merit itself is a class-formed currency (Bourdieu, 1986).

My own journey has underlined this tension. When I left China for France in 2005, my mother's life savings – the equivalent of a modest €10,000 – felt both generous and precarious. In Lyon, even a simple sandwich cost what I'd spent on a week's worth of food in Kunming. This dissonance between my family's sacrifices and the cost of living in Europe revealed how financial barriers are embodied – a daily negotiation of anxiety and guilt that no statistic captures.

But the commodification of British academia goes beyond fees. It reduces education to a transactional service, where students are 'customers' and diversity is a branding tool. This cooperative logic positions students from the global South as revenue generators rather than intellectual contributors. Their presence is welcomed, but their epistemologies – unless neatly packaged for Western consumption – remain marginal.

The ability to pursue education in the United Kingdom is largely confined to a privileged minority in China, whose families possess significant *economic capital* to afford tuition and living costs. Beyond financial means, these students inherit *cultural capital* – advanced through elite schooling, private tutoring, and extracurricular training – and *social capital*, cultivated via familial networks and global exposure through travel or exchanges. As Pierre Bourdieu (1986) observed, such pre-existing advantages are compounded by institutional systems that convert these forms of capital into *symbolic capital*: markers of prestige and legitimacy.

Graduating from a 'prestigious British university' amplifies this dynamic. The UK degree operates as a globally recognised form of *symbolic capital*, enhancing graduates' status in China's labour market, where Western credentials are often valorised. This reinforces their elite positioning within Chinese society, perpetuating cycles of social stratification.

Yet in the United Kingdom, these students occupy a paradoxical space. Despite their acquired credentials, they remain on the periphery of British social hierarchies, where ethnic and cultural differences dilute the symbolic power of their capital. Bourdieu's framework reveals how capital's value is context-dependent: while their UK education strengthens their standing in China, systemic biases in the UK labour market – rooted in racialised class structures – limit its efficacy. Thus, the very system that elevates their status domestically underscores their marginalisation abroad, illustrating how education perpetuates global inequities even as it promises mobility.

While Chinese and British students navigate different socio-cultural landscapes, the structural barriers faced by working-class individuals – whether from rural China or post-industrial Liverpool – are strikingly similar. In both contexts, the divide between those from affluent, established families and those from working-class backgrounds stems from the same neoliberal machinery that converts pre-existing economic and cultural advantages – elite education, inherited networks, global mobility – into *symbolic capital* (Bourdieu, 1986), reinforcing hierarchies while framing inequality as a matter of individual 'merit'. A student from China's urban elite, groomed by costly extracurricular investments, and a student from Liverpool, without generational access to internships or tuition support, both face a rigged game. Their trajectories are shaped less by effort than by structural asymmetries: who can afford to play by the rules of a marketised education system. In this sense, neoliberalism functions as a global script. It naturalises class divisions by conflating privilege with 'potential', ensuring that mobility remains the exception rather than the norm.

Again, the neoliberal rhetoric of 'fair opportunity' and 'free movement' seemed to be reserved for a select few, while significant barriers remained for those who didn't start with a 'high bar' or who didn't fit neatly into the global narrative of privilege and mobility. Ultimately, the high tuition fees and the corporate, neoliberal values and corresponding management practices of British academia not only bypass genuine intellectual and personal growth, which for me is the core value and purpose of higher education itself, but also serve as a means of reinforcing social classification rather than helping to redress it. Gramsci's insight into the relationship between knowledge and social structures and Bourdieu's insight into social capital and distinction resonate here: 'Knowledge is a social construct that serves to legitimise social structures' (Bourdieu, 1984; Heywood, 1994: 85).

After several years of working as a full-time academic, I came to realise that the UK academic system is deeply entangled in a 'global network' (this 'globe' refers mainly to the Anglophone and recently emerging 'nation-states' that embrace neoliberal values and logics) driven by rankings, metrics, and assessment frameworks such as Times Higher Education (THE). The World University Rankings shape every aspect of the academic landscape. These frameworks play a crucial role in the UK academic landscape, providing benchmarks for excellence and guiding funding and policy decisions. Disciplines that attract funding or measurable 'impact' are prioritised, while others are dismissed as quaint relics. Departments are seen less as guardians of knowledge and more as economic units contributing to institutional visibility and profit. High tuition fees and funding mechanisms that favour certain disciplines and types of research over others are, in my view, increasingly interfering with the fundamental purpose and meaning of education and knowledge, turning education into a training programme in exchange for short-term profit.

An interlocking system of power

Living in Liverpool as an academic, I gradually came to terms with the contradictions embedded in the ideals of 'academic neutrality' and 'liberal freedom'. These concepts, often presented as universal, turned out to be conditioned by geopolitical power and institutional self-interest, with two global crises crystallising this disillusionment.

The COVID-19 pandemic, first, exposed how 'neutrality' fractures under ideological pressure. As a Chinese living abroad, I witnessed Western media reduce China's pandemic response to a caricature, flattening complex public health measures into a simplistic 'authoritarian vs. free world' narrative.

Then, in 2023, the Israel-Palestine conflict laid bare the limits of 'free speech' in liberal institutions. On UK and US campuses, critiques of Israeli military actions were stifled under accusations of antisemitism, while Palestinian civilian suffering was side-lined as a 'niche' or 'divisive' issue. This selective enforcement of 'open debate' – where power dictates whose pain is legible – forced a reckoning: the 'liberal world' champions universal rights in theory, yet in practice, it arbitrates whose humanity merits more protection.

These events revealed a recurring pattern: ideals like fairness and freedom often function not as principles but as tools of power. Neutrality, I realised, is a privilege reserved for those already aligned with dominant systems.

My disillusionment with the rhetoric of 'academic neutrality' and 'fair opportunity' in Britain mirrored my earlier conclusions about France's proclaimed 'liberty, equality, fraternity'. After a decade in France as an Asian student navigating its marginalised communities, I saw how these ideals obscured entrenched inequities. In the United Kingdom, however, class divisions felt starker. Unchecked corporate power and the absence of meaningful government intervention had widened the gulf between elites and the working class, rendering the contrasts absurdly drastic.

Through years of living experience, research, and reflection in both France and the United Kingdom, I began to realise how deep the ideological dissonance really is, going far beyond what I had initially observed. My experiences in France illuminated these contradictions, but my time in the United Kingdom peeled back even deeper layers of the proclaimed ideals of diversity and fair opportunity that capitalist neoliberalism so often promotes. In fact, despite the rhetoric of inclusivity and social progress, I witnessed how marginalised groups – particularly the working class and migrant workers – were further marginalised by rigid social hierarchies and an entrenched class system based on economic privilege and racial/ethnic prejudice. These groups were not only excluded but often stigmatised and made into projections of society's fears, their difference reinforced by neoliberal policies that championed individual success and market-driven values.

My experiences as a 'woman of colour' in British society, even within academia, have consistently aligned with what bell hooks (1984:51) described as 'white supremacist capitalist patriarchy'. The interconnected systems of power and domination that hooks articulated from her perspective as a black woman in the United States clearly resonate with my own journey. These systems collectively maintain societal structures that benefit a select few, and my experiences have consistently confirmed the reality hooks described – where my gender, racial identity, and social position often collide with the barriers of this interlocking system, both explicitly and implicitly.

Interestingly, my reflections have also led me to rethink the dynamics I once took for granted in my research on Chinese rock music, a field I studied and largely embraced as both a researcher and a passionate listener, especially in my teens and early twenties. Although the notion of race is not applied in the same way in China as it is in Western contexts, it has become clear to me that economic, gender, marginalisation, and hierarchical oppression are still at work, particularly in the context of China's reform era. Within Chinese society, these intersecting oppressions manifest as a unique interlocking system of domination – a unique fusion of what I call imperialist supremacist feudal patriarchy and what hooks calls 'imperialist white supremacist capitalist patriarchy' (hooks, 2004: 29).

Racism or colourism, as understood in Western contexts, does not fit neatly into China's social stratification. Discrimination does, however, manifest itself through regional and ethnic bias. Rural migrants, for example, face stigmatisation linked to perceived 'backwardness' – their labour-weathered skin, dialects, and customs are labelled 'uncivilised' in urban centres. Despite constitutional equality, ethnic minorities face systemic inequality in education, employment, and media representation. These prejudices, while not rooted in skin colour per se, function in a similar way: they naturalise exclusion by conflating identity with worth.

This hybrid system of domination mentioned above shapes the daily lives of individuals living in China and is made even more apparent by global events such as the COVID-19 pandemic, because it placed China in a wider geopolitical context and highlighted its connection to wider interlocking systems of power. These global events demonstrate how global structures of power and local modes of control intersect in very tangible ways.

Looking back, I now realise that the world of rock music, including Chinese rock or *Yaogun*, which I had once idealised as rebellious and liberating 'for all', was not immune to the same dynamics. It too had a structure of domination that reflected wider social norms. Rock music has historically been a male-dominated, often sexist domain, marred by scandals involving rockers' abuse of 'groupies' and exploitation by major record companies targeting individuals of racial, ethnic, or gender identities for profit. The Chinese rock scene was even more male-dominated, with only a few exceptions of female members and bands. Almost all the 'recognised' rock critics, including the scholars who wrote extensively about rock and *Yaogun*, were also male.

At the time, I was unaware of these underlying forces, captivated by the sound and energy of the music. My more recent reflections, however, reveal that even within what appeared to be a space for genuine rebellion, the very systems I now recognise – the interlocking forces of racism, capitalism, patriarchy, and feudal/imperial domination – were present and exerting their influence in subtle but significant ways that profoundly affected my journey.

The unfinished finale

From 'me' to 'us' – Metamorphosis of cross-cultural identity integration

Throughout the first part of this book, I situated my observations, reflections, and experiences within the world of Chinese rock and mainland China – the cultural phenomenon known as *Yaogun*. The aim was not simply to recount the history of rock music in China or to provide a cultural narrative from my personal perspective. Rather, in the words of sinologist Jean-François Billeter (2000:18), my aim was to use *Yaogun* to illuminate 'what was ultimately decisive in the chain of cause and effect' in the formation of a nation's identity at a time of profound change in Chinese society, and to illustrate how its journey interacted closely with the wider global geopolitical power dynamics and with those who listened to and related to it as individuals. For me, rock music, an imported genre from the West, became a perfect prism through which to examine China's uneasy relationship with what Gregory Lee (2002:74) calls the 'spectre of the West'– a spectre that embodies both the allure and the anxiety of capitalist modernity.

This 'spectre' crystallised through my dual journey: interrogating *Yaogun*'s development while navigating different cultural, social, and ideological landscapes. In the end, it materialised as neoliberal capitalism – a system that peddles myths of limitless opportunity and progress, even as it entrenches the inequalities it claims to dismantle. The result is a world in which progress is commodified, expansion is limitless, and social hierarchies are repackaged as meritocratic inevitabilities. At its core, neoliberalism is a paradox: a rhetoric of liberation that shackles, a language of openness that segregates.

For China, the twentieth century unmasked the 'spectre's' contradictions. The same ideologies that promised modernity also entrenched dependence on extractive global systems, replicating colonial patterns of dominance over the global South.

Yaogun was born in the 1980s, a period marked by China's reopening to global influences after the long shadow of the Cultural Revolution. It was an era marked by an eagerness to redefine what it meant to be Chinese in the context of 'modernisation', a term which until then had been largely synonymous with Westernisation (Lee, 2012a). Deng Xiaoping's vision – a 'capitalist under socialist state control' model – allowed for economic liberalisation while ostensibly preserving the ideological principles of socialism. It was in this space of ideological negotiation that *Yaogun* took root – as both a cultural import and an attempt to redefine 'modern' in uniquely Chinese terms.

The rise of *Yaogun* during China's reform era offers a critical lens to examine the nation's uneasy quest to forge a 'modern socialist national identity' – a project paradoxically dependent on the Western frameworks it seeks to reject. This tension stems from a broader historical watershed: the Opium War and subsequent colonial humiliations dismantled imperial China's insularity and forced a century of defensive modernisation. After 1949, the PRC's socialist vision aimed to transcend capitalist models, but capitalist neoliberal globalisation forced a pragmatic adoption of Western norms, technologies, and cultural forms. Emerging from this duality, *Yaogun* embodies the contradictions of a nation-state negotiating self-definition amid borrowed ideologies.

China's post-reform generation grew up reciting the CCP's Four Modernisations (四个现代化) – a state blueprint for transforming agriculture, industry, defence, and science/technology into the pillars of a 'modern' nation. This framework prioritised material progress over ideological purity and catalysed China's rapid rise as a global economic power. But its legacy goes beyond GDP figures: it reshaped societal values, elevating STEM disciplines and instrumental rationality as markers of 'modernity'. Universities, reflecting state priorities, poured resources into technical fields while marginalising the humanities – a trend I witnessed first-hand in both Chinese and British academia.

This institutional bias towards quantifiable outcomes reflects a deeper paradox. While China's modernisation rhetoric champions the neoliberal ideal of the 'self-made individual' (Harvey, 2005), its citizens navigate a system that assigns personal worth to economic productivity. Autonomy in this context becomes a double bind: individuals are tasked with self-optimisation in a society that structurally limits dissent, creativity, and non-conformity.

Modernity here reveals its contradiction: a collectivist project sold in the language of individual agency, yet one that demands conformity to state-sanctioned pragmatism. For many Chinese, being 'modern' means negotiating this dissonance – performing neoliberal self-reliance while longing for spaces where identity isn't dictated by the utilitarian calculation. There seems to be a fundamental structural contradiction between this model of autonomy and the traditional Chinese cultural and social framework, which has always emphasised collective harmony and family obligations over individual voices. My experiences navigating social contexts and living in China and Europe have made me more aware that this contradiction is so deeply embedded in the social fabric and collective mindset in China. So much so that even after two decades abroad, I still struggle with tensions between personal will and family/institutional expectations and norms. Also, being an 'only child' (独生子女) only intensifies this pressure – one that weighs heavily on many in China's 'only child' generation.

What does it mean to be a 'modern Chinese' on a personal level? 'Speaking English or more than one language? Wearing clothes designed by stylists? Using multiple personal pronouns other than he or she? Learning about modern psychology and 'symbolically killing one's parents'? Practicing 'self-love'? Being able to speak as an 'independent, critical citizen'? What exactly does it mean to be 'modern'? And why has it been such a crucial theme for the individuals and nation of China for about a century, especially since the 1980s? After all, is it all about 'self-determination and self-esteem', whether for an individual, or for a new nation breaking with its heavy feudal history and seeking to represent its people as an entity? These are also questions I have asked myself during my academic interrogation of Chinese rock and over the past two decades of living in China, France, and the United Kingdom.

To forge an authentic identity in 'modernity', *Yaogun* and I – like much of post-reform China – must navigate a paradox: we rely on Western frameworks (terms, ideologies, metrics) even as we resist their hegemony. This duality reflects broader cultural phenomena in post-reform China – literature, film, art – that borrow from capitalist modernity while critiquing its encroachment. Our rebellion is existential, rejecting both Western cultural hegemony and the authoritarian pragmatism that enables it. *Yaogun* thus becomes both mirror and microcosm: it reflects China's struggle to commodify 'progress' without undermining its socialist exceptionalism, just as it exposes the personal turmoil of a generation raised between neoliberal individualism and collectivist dogma.

The 'invisible Chinese rock', or the silence of China

Reflecting on the questions raised at the beginning of Part I: Why has *Yaogun*, despite its vitality in the 1980s and 1990s and its role in awakening personal consciousness and dissent within China, remained largely invisible on the global stage? For whom does it really exist? These questions go beyond the music to explore deeper tensions in China's cultural geopolitics. Even as the nation has risen economically, its cultural exports – especially those that challenge state or market orthodoxies – have struggled to penetrate local and global gatekeeping.

This invisibility cannot simply be reduced to language barriers or artistic merit. Anglophone rock, after all, has crossed borders effortlessly, unbound by linguistic familiarity. Nor is it a failure to 'resonate' – *Yaogun*'s themes largely resonate with the classic rock canon. Rather, this marginalisation exposes the asymmetries of cultural agency: whose dissent is amplified, whose creativity is legible. Global recognition depends not only on artistic integrity but also on geopolitical hierarchies that privilege certain narratives while side-lining others. *Yaogun*'s absence from the world stage is less an accident than an inscription of power – a reminder that cultural exchange is curated by those who hold the keys.

Yaogun was not merely a musical import from the West; it became a vessel for collective aspirations and a means to articulate individual voices within a society shaped by decades of communist ideology and the deeply embedded Confucian mindset of collectivism. The sounds, aesthetics, and ethos of rock music sharply diverged from the collectivist values of both revolutionary and ancient China, embracing a spirit of individualism – an 'unconventional independence' that felt foreign, and at times unsettling, to many. Yet it was precisely this divergence that made *Yaogun* a symbol of yearning – a voice for a generation caught at the crossroads between tradition and modernity, between community-focused socialist ideals and pragmatic, individual ambitions.

Yaogun's trajectory reveals a paradox of constrained emergence. While Western rock music – often mythologised as a catalyst for civil rights and countercultural movements – operated within societies that granted relative cultural autonomy, *Yaogun* took shape within an authoritarian system that allowed dissent only within strict limits. Its existence depended on a state-sanctioned 'controlled modernity' that allowed rock to function as a pressure valve for urban youth, but never as a vehicle for systemic critique.

This institutional balancing act defined *Yaogun*'s limitations. Unlike its Western counterparts, it lacked the grassroots infrastructure or mass mobilisation potential to evolve beyond subcultural status. Meanwhile, China's post-1990s market reforms further diluted its subversive edge. Consumerism co-opted rebellion into a commodified aesthetic, reducing *Yaogun*'s once-potent dissent to a soundtrack for individualistic escapism. By the 2000s, its domestic resonance had waned, overshadowed by a neoliberal narrative that recast 'freedom' as consumer choice rather than collective emancipation. Ultimately, *Yaogun*'s arc reflects a broader tension: how cultural resistance navigates systems that simultaneously enable and neutralise its transformative potential.

The marginalisation of *Yaogun* on global digital platforms such as Spotify and Apple Music cannot be separated from the geopolitical undercurrents that shape technological and cultural ecosystems. Often framed as neutral arbiters of 'global culture', these platforms are often embedded in power structures that reflect US-China tensions, trade wars, and competing visions of digital sovereignty. Content moderation policies, algorithmic curation, and licensing agreements – ostensibly technical decisions – are increasingly weaponised in broader struggles for ideological influence and market dominance. For China, this means that its cultural output faces double barriers: restrictive domestic internet governance and exclusionary Western gatekeeping that dismisses non-Anglophone creativity as niche or suspect.

Meanwhile, this systemic omission underscores a deeper dynamic: Chinese cultural production is deemed legible only when filtered through Western frameworks of 'authenticity'. Such gatekeeping epitomises Western cultural imperialism – the hegemony that dictates whose creativity is valorised as 'universal' and whose is relegated to the exotic or threatening. When China enters the global discourse, it is confined to Orientalist binaries: romanticised as an 'ancient civilisation' or weaponised as an 'authoritarian threat'. Rock music, existential questioning, and counterculural dissent – hallmarks of 'modernity' when performed in the West – are stripped of their legitimacy when they emerge from China, either rendered invisible or recast as imitation, or reinterpreted through the Western-centric perspective.

This gatekeeping perpetuates a colonial logic. Just as nineteenth-century imperialism reduced non-Western societies to static curiosities, today's cultural imperialism demands that China remain a silent relic or a threatening disrupter – never an equal contributor to global modernity. *Yaogun*'s marginalisation thus reflects China's broader struggle: to assert agency in a world where cultural capital remains concentrated in Euro-American hands, and where deviation from Western scripts invites rejection or demonisation.

In the end, examining Chinese rock reveals the broader, more intricate journey of China itself – a journey marked by constant negotiation between embracing, rejecting, and integrating external influences. Chinese rock embodies a desire for cultural rejuvenation that both draws from and diverges from external frameworks. The paradox of striving for 'modernity' while seeking autonomy and independence, and simultaneously asserting a cultural identity deeply rooted in China's heritage, is not unique to Chinese rock; it highlights China's ongoing quest for self-definition in a world largely shaped by Western paradigms and the ideologies of capitalist, neoliberal values.

From 'me' to 'us': Standing on the periphery together

When I reflect on the struggles of *Yaogun*, or modern China as a new nation-state, I see two seemingly different but fundamentally intertwined processes. Both are united by a common pursuit: the desire to establish autonomy and an authentic identity – a sort of sovereignty. This pursuit, however, is marked by an uneasy negotiation: using the language and frameworks of external influences, while striving to preserve a rootedness in their own inheritance, a civilisational tradition that is an essential part of their current existence, carrying the weight of a long history.

In this pursuit, I also see my own reflection – a fragment of the same yearning. I was a young Chinese girl coming of age in a society undergoing rapid transformation, discovering rock music, and feeling awakened by the sheer energy of drumbeats, the electric guitar riffs, and the bold lyrics that spoke directly to my soul. I was enchanted by the myth of rock and *Yaogun* – a music form that was 'subversive, revolutionary', singing for the 'powerless and suffocated', fighting for a broader justice that seemed elusive but necessary. Through this music, I felt as though I was finding my voice – a raw, unpolished, but determined voice. It was within this idealised 'bubble' that I began the journey to carve out my path as an 'autonomous individual with integrity', leaving behind my home and my 'motherland', setting out to navigate the once-mystified realms of 'enlightened Europe' and 'liberal England', which I had seen as the 'model societies' that promised freedom and understanding.

Like *Yaogun*, I faced the pressures of navigating multiple norms and surveillance structures, both from my immediate family and my 'motherland', burdened with heavy historical and ideological legacies that seemed to suffocate individuality. The expectations weighed heavily on me – rooted in a strong collective and patriarchal social mindset, and the relentless pursuit of perfection as dictated by parental and institutional standards. In a rapidly transforming society that is obsessed with neoliberal-oriented meritocracy, there was an unwavering belief that 'progress and success' were the only keys to personal fulfilment, despite individual differences. In the meantime, living abroad as a Chinese female student/scholar, there were also pressures and challenges from my 'guest houses' in France and the United Kingdom. These societies, with the solid capitalist, neoliberal patriarchal social order and systemic social inequalities – including racial, ethnic, gender, and class biases – often isolate individuals, regarded as 'agents of social labour', leaving them as detached atoms without space to build meaningful connections and nurture bonds that are essential for healthy and thriving human relationships.

My journey towards self-construction and the forging of an autonomous personal identity – or, in Carl Jung's (1968) terms, 'one's true self' – began as a Chinese girl born and raised in the residential quarters of a military hospital. This journey unfolded in a China transitioning from a post-Cultural Revolution collectivist model to a society still under socialist state control, yet increasingly shaped by market forces, neoliberal values, and consumerism. While collective social consciousness remained deeply ingrained, new currents of individual aspiration emerged. For me, navigating this shifting landscape meant balancing personal agency against the enduring weight of collective expectations and normalisation.

And yet, when I moved to France and later to the United Kingdom, I found myself in a new struggle: an unsettling sense of 'losing my identity' and all the social credentials I had built up in China. I was being constantly 'othered' by the interconnected network of power, experiencing a deep sense of isolation and loneliness in a post-industrial and neoliberal society – as an 'atomised individual' (Taylor, 1985), struggling to find 'true belonging' and constantly feeling peripheral: in society, in academia, in my own skin.

As time went on, the struggles of *Yaogun* and myself all began to make a certain sense, and it provoked a persistent question I had been asking myself: is this the only way forward? Once deeply influenced by the myth of rock and Enlightenment ideals, I resonated with Berman's radical self – grappling with the tension between individual identity and the broader community, navigating both emancipation and alienation in the face of modernity. Yet, through years of traversing the landscapes of China, France, and the United Kingdom, I gradually came to terms with Jungian individuation and the concept of a more holistic 'Self' (Jung, 1968), which does not seek liberation through detachment but through integration – both within the psyche and in relation to the world. In Jung's terms, it is an ongoing process of aligning the ego with the deeper, more holistic Self, fostering a sense of wholeness that transcends external validation while remaining deeply engaged with the social fabric.

I gradually realised that it's not only about 'me' but also about 'us', and it was only by recognising the 'non-ego-centred me' that I finally found a sense of belonging – an integration of all the 'other' inseparable elements that make up 'me'. This realisation brought me relief as well as hope for a 'third way' beyond the 'compliance or resistance' pattern – a way rooted in common ground, in a shared future, and no more from a dichotomy of 'me' and 'other', of 'us' and 'them', as they are ultimately interdependent and inseparable. At a time when the world is increasingly divided, defined by oppositions, and marked by the looming threat of self-destruction through advanced technologies and nuclear power, this realisation seems more relevant.

My thoughts turn to the people I met during my years abroad – neighbours in the HLM complex buildings in the suburbs of Lyon, from all corners of the world, with their own stories, often not easy ones. Fellow students who worked part-time to sustain their studies and everyday life, migrant workers whose invisible labour helped keep society going. In the end, I realised that we were not so different after all. Despite our seemingly different skin colours, cultural backgrounds, languages, habits, and social roles, we were fundamentally connected by our common status on the 'periphery' – by our common struggle to be rendered invisible in one way or another.

In this struggle, the dedication in a book I found by chance – abandoned on a 'free books' shelf in the basement of an office building (what an irony of life!) – began to resonate deeply. The dedication read: 'Dedicated to the poor and oppressed women of the world, whose anonymous struggles are the building blocks of a new society.' The book was called *Development, Crises and Alternative Visions: Third World Women's Perspectives* (Sen and Grown, 1987). The words found me in a moment of clarity. They illuminated an unexpected connection between my experiences and those of countless 'others' who share the world's margins, who, like me, are struggling to forge their own identities and move towards the 'realisation of the self' within a vast, intertwined network of forces, under the constraints of societal and structural norms.

I've come to realise that the invisibility of Chinese rock is not unlike the invisibility of women as a constructed social gender throughout history – they both share the absence of subjectivity based on self-determination and self-reliance. Ultimately, all these invisible individuals, rendered invisible by their peripheral position – *Yaogun*, Women, the 'Third World', or 'global South' – share a common ground. They are united by the experience of being on the periphery, of feeling marginalised.

Meanwhile, my personal journey – from Kunming to Beijing, from Beijing to France, from France to the United Kingdom, from student to doctoral candidate to academic – also reflects my cross-cultural identity integration. It is a long process, a process of 'encountering, embracing, doubting, rejecting, transforming, integrating'. Looking back, this journey has involved integrating many aspects of my life: personal choices, unpredictable encounters, moving between different countries, navigating different social contexts, with intellectual, spiritual, and behavioural transformations. Although challenging, it has been a constructive path towards the 'self-asserting' and 'self-realisation' I've been seeking for most of my adult life.

Now, after more than two decades of this ongoing journey, I have come to realise that there was probably not 'one, true self' but 'many, delusional selves'. These 'delusional selves' 'appeared' in different stages of my life and might have dissolved over time, but in a way they never really 'disappeared' either as they never 'existed' as some inherent entities to begin with. The core insight I have gained from this long journey is that there is no 'solid and substantial self' that could be claimed as 'personal identity'; instead, there is an ever-changing, composite, fluid sense of identity that I have experienced as 'I' or 'me', and this realisation resonates deeply with the Buddhist philosophy of 'non-self' (*anattā*) or 'emptiness' (*śūnyatā*) (Bodhi, 2000; Nāgārjuna, 1995).

Standing together on the periphery remains a vital step in reimagining identity – not merely as solidarity, but as a radical interrogation of how we exist within and beyond oppressive systems. Power structures thrive on enforcing 'difference', coercing us into rigid categories of belonging. Yet the periphery offers an alternative: the freedom of *invisibility*, a release from ego-driven identities, or, as Buddhist philosophy frames it, an 'empty self' brimming with possibilities. Here, the periphery offered glimpses of a world freed from binaries – a possibility to reconstitute *self* and *other* not through exclusionary labels, but through mutual vulnerability and interdependence born of shared systemic exclusion.

In those margins – where the myth of 'enlightened' individualism cracked under the weight of my stolen wallet and the stones thrown by immigrant children – I began to grasp what Édouard Glissant (1997) called *relation*. Not a kinship born of sameness, but a fringed, necessary bond between those who have survived a shared exclusion. This was no utopia. It was a reckoning: Lyon's periphery did not transcend hierarchy, but it did force me to confront how race, class, and colonialism warped identities, including my own. The same hierarchies I'd fled in China wore different masks here, but their foundations felt familiar.

In this liminal space, I did not find a 'new humanity'. Instead, I unearthed the tools I'd lacked in Beijing: the clarity to see systems, rather than 'self' or 'other', as the architects of division. The periphery did not answer who I was – it asked instead what I might become if I stopped clinging to the identities that power had inscribed on me.

A cross-cultural identity process: Transcending the 'box', constantly in making

Throughout this book, my journey has been an exploration of the interconnected paths of Chinese rock music, my sense of self across different cultural, social, and political frameworks, and the process of integrating a cross-cultural identity that turns out to be fluid and constantly in the making. These threads have illuminated a broader quest altogether: what it means for a person or a nation to build an identity amid rapid, profound changes and challenges?

Between modernity and fragmentation

China's struggle to reconcile its historical and cultural heritage with a capitalist, neoliberal narrative of modernity reflects a global reckoning. Today, a new revolution driven by AI, biotechnology, and digital integration threatens to dissolve the boundaries between human and machine, self and algorithm. Like the paradox of Chinese rock, which oscillated between rebellion and assimilation, this moment demands that we confront the double-edged potential of technological progress: will it further fracture identities or forge new paradigms of thought and action, and thus new possibilities related to the very idea of identity?

The journey of Chinese rock – a peripheral art form that negotiates both the internal Chinese systemic oppression and the Western narratives of cultural imperialism – reflects the broader tensions facing nation-states and individuals alike today. The nation-state, within the capitalist, neoliberal framework, functions as a 'collective ego' based on defensive self-protection and limitless self-expansion, which thrives on distinction and differentiation: us/them, East/West, 'upper'/'lower', 'backward'/'advanced'. These binaries, often weaponised through ethno-nationalism, sexism, communalism, and territorialism, fuel the very conflicts they claim to resolve. My research on Chinese rock has shown how cultural resistance, even when expressed in the 'other language' of rock, punk, underground movements, or acts of decolonisation, risks replicating the hierarchies it seeks to dismantle.

Disillusionment as revelation

The second half of this book traces my lived disenchantment – from the illusionary 'elite centre' to Beijing's male-dominated rock scenes, to Lyon's post-colonial peripheries and Liverpool's neoliberal contradictions. Each space exposed systemic hierarchies at the intersections of race, gender, and class that privileged a select group of people while rendering certain bodies invisible. But the mechanism of rendering invisibility became a lens: stripped of the privileges of academic titles and social capital, I saw how power operates globally, adapting its mask to local contexts.

In China, my identity as a 'rebellious' woman in the rock music circle marked me as the 'other' in the male-dominated world; my social role as a female, single academic marked me as an unwelcome outsider ('the third sex') in the expectations of patriarchal society. In Europe, my ethnic and social background collided with colonial legacies, reducing me to an 'Asian immigrant' navigating glass doors in housing, employment, and bureaucracy. These experiences, overlaid with my study of Buddhism and Taoism, crystallised a core revelation for me: the 'self' we cling to – whether national, regional, ethnic, gendered, or academic – is a construct shaped by individual greed, fear, and the capitulation to interlocking systems of power that profit from division.

Towards fluid belonging: Transcending the 'box'

Ancient Eastern philosophies compelled me to question the 'labels' we associate with selfhood – constructs that capitalism, neoliberalism, communalism, and ethno-nationalism peddle as security through exclusionary belonging. Yet this security, rooted in self-centred insulation and Othering, remains a constructed illusion. My journey – from the residential blocks of Kunming to the dormitories of Beijing and the HLMs of Lyon – revealed a shared fragility: globally, the most marginalised exist at the intersection of race/ethnicity, gender, and class. It also brought to light an embodied insight: only through shared precarity with those Othered could I begin to dissolve the divisive 'box', and to embrace cross-cultural becoming – a fluid negotiation of belonging and resistance.

To 'transcend the box' is not to reject identity, but to treat it as a *process* of negotiation. Drawing on Taoist *zìrán* (自然, 'self-so-ness') and Buddhist *pratītyasamutpāda* (dependent origination), I propose identity as a fluid interplay between local agency and global hegemonies – a constant remaking amid the currents of power.

This is not utopian or another myth. The peripheries I inhabited – Beijing's underground venues, Lyon's HLMs – taught me that systemic exclusion binds us in shared precarity. Yet within this precarity lies potential: by rejecting fixed categories, we destabilise the binaries and distinctions that construct and maintain hegemony.

Finally, the cross-cultural identity I propose is not a goal but a practice – a constant unlearning of the hierarchies inscribed in language, borders, presumed nationalities, titles, and algorithms. It asks: What might we become if we released the need to belong to a fixed 'label', family, nation, community, system, and instead belonged through shared vulnerability with anyone who crosses this shared path in the making?

My journey remains unfinished, as all genuine *becoming* must. It is a path of constant negotiation: with the structures that seek to define me, with the borders (real and imagined) that I was told to police, and with the selves to which I cling out of greed, fear, or habit. To embrace a cross-cultural identity is to dwell in the liminal – to find fluidity in the space between fixed categories, where 'home' becomes neither a place nor a label but a practice of *not belonging*.

It is here, in the interplay of autonomy and interdependence, that I encounter the paradox of identity: it is fluid yet rooted, empty of permanence yet charged with potential. The peripheries I have inhabited – Kunming, Beijing, Lyon, Liverpool – have taught me that to 'transcend the box' is not to erase difference, but to refuse to militarise it into a rigid, ideological fixation on capture or manipulation. It's about embracing the feeling of 'not being at home anywhere', but at the same time 'being at home everywhere'. To distil the essence of this journey into one line:

> **We are dancing together on this unfinished journey – distinct, yet inseparable.**

Suggested projects, assignments, and discussion questions

1. Comparative analysis of rock (or other) cultures through case studies

Aim:

To critically examine Chinese and Western rock music (or other cultures) as cultural lenses that reflect distinct socio-political discourses, individual identities, and cultural narratives.

Suggested components (using rock music as an example):

- Select one or more representative Chinese and Western rock songs or live performances (e.g., Cui Jian's 'Nothing to My Name', Bruce Springsteen's 'Born in the USA').
- Conduct a comparative analysis focusing on:
- Lyrical content and thematic concerns
- Historical and socio-political contexts
- Symbolic elements in performance and presentation

- Cultural impact and reception in their respective societies
- Consider how these works engage with issues of identity, power, resistance, and/or commodification.

Assignment prompt (suggestion):

Write a short critical essay, or collaborate in group-based class discussions, addressing the following:

- How does each selected song or performance reflect internal societal elements (e.g., post-Mao reform-era China versus Cold War-era America)?
- What connections can be drawn between these works and broader global dynamics of power and transnational cultural flows?
- How do structural elements – such as historical context, socio-political conditions, cultural values, prevailing ideologies, and collective mentalities – influence the creative processes and thematic expressions of these musicians?

2. Autoethnographic narrative project (e.g., autoethnographic multimedia portfolio)

Aim:

To explore the interplay between self-perception and social/structural influences. Students will practice reflective engagement with personal experiences that resonate with collective identities, shared social issues, or broader cultural dynamics, using autoethnography as a method of inquiry.

Suggested components:

- **Autoethnographic Essay:** Compose a short autoethnographic essay (1,500–2,000 words) based on a musical or cultural scene with which you have had personal involvement (e.g., a local indie scene, a hip-hop collective, K-pop fandom).

Guiding questions: Personal and cultural reflection

o Narrate a personal experience within a specific cultural setting (e.g., attending a live music event, participating in a fandom, engaging with a traditional or contemporary cultural community).

o How did this experience shape your understanding of self, your values, and your sense of belonging?

o Employ autoethnographic methods by weaving together personal narrative (e.g., storytelling, emotions, reflections, and impacts on your life) with cultural analysis (e.g., socio-historical context, media and technology influence, cultural heritage, and relevant social theories).

Creative component:

Complement your essay with a curated creative element such as:

o A track playlist
o A photo-essay or visual montage
o A short podcast (e.g., ten to fifteen minutes)

This component should evoke and illustrate key themes and moments in your narrative.

Reflection commentary:

o How did your participation in this cultural practice inform your self-identity and values?

o   In what ways does your personal experience echo or diverge from Lei Peng's exploration of her cross-cultural identity through Chinese rock?

Note to Students: This assignment encourages both critical and creative thinking. You are invited to bring your lived experience into dialogue with cultural theory. Consider the broader significance of your narrative: what does your story tell us about the relationship between a culture scene, identity, and society?

3. Critical engagement project: Identity, knowledge production, and cultural politics

Aim:

To critically explore Chinese rock music as an example of a 'periphery culture' within the current global power structure. The primary objective is to examine how this cultural phenomenon both shapes and is shaped by internal and global geopolitical dynamics. The project will also address the deep-seated influence of cultural imperialism, colonial heritage, and internal cultural restrictions in knowledge production and dissemination. Central to the discussion is the representation conundrum, where peripheral cultures like Chinese rock are often distorted or marginalised within dominant global narratives. Moreover, the project will investigate how Chinese traditional collectivist mindsets and ideological constraints imposed by the Chinese authorities shape the production, reception, and representation of such music within both national and global contexts.

Suggested components:

The project will involve group discussions or debates, encouraging the exploration of diverse perspectives. Students will critically engage with how Chinese rock, as a periphery cultural form – or other peripheral cultures related to students' own backgrounds or experiences – navigates the complex intersections of global power, cultural imperialism, and historical legacies, as well as internal ideological and cultural restrictions. The focus will be on understanding how these influences affect the representation and reception of such cultures within the global context.

Guiding questions:

- How might academic studies of non-Western cultural phenomena (such as Chinese rock) unintentionally reinforce notions of 'otherness'? In what ways can scholars critically reflect on their positionality and adopt inclusive methodologies to resist reproducing these dynamics?

- How does consumerism either dilute or amplify the subversive potential of Chinese rock music? Consider case studies such as music festivals, streaming platforms, variety shows, or digital media influence. How do other cultural forms – like fashion, film, contemporary art, street art, or even grassroots activism – face similar dynamics of commodification and commodified rebellion?

- Can autoethnography challenge Western-centric academic frameworks? Why or why not? How does this methodology allow for a deeper understanding of cross-cultural identities, and what are its limitations?

- In what ways do cultural imperialism, colonial legacies, and internal restrictions (e.g., Chinese collectivist mindsets and

ideological constraints from the Chinese authorities) influence the way Chinese rock is produced, consumed, and represented globally?
- How do global power dynamics influence the perception of non-Western cultural expressions in the global music scene? What are the consequences for the authenticity and autonomy of these cultural forms?
- What role does representation play in shaping the global reception of peripheral cultures? How do misrepresentations or the lack of representation affect the identity and agency of these cultures?
- What are examples of other cultural forms (such as digital subcultures, independent cinema, or alternative literature) that have similar subversive potential? How do these forms navigate the pressures of neo-liberal globalisation, commodification, and cultural appropriation?

Notes

1. These extracts of lyrics are translated from Chinese to English by the author from songs featured in the album *Shameful Being Left Alone* and *N.43 Baojiajie Road*.
2. These extracts of lyrics are translated from Chinese to English by the author from Cui Jian's song 'Nothing to My Name' 《一无所有》.
3. The Long March 长征 (1934–1936) was a strategic retreat by the Chinese Communist Party's Red Army (CCP) (红军), led by figures like Mao Zedong, during the Chinese Civil War. Covering 6,000 miles, it aimed to escape KMT forces (the Nationalist Kuomintang led by Chiang Kai-shek蒋介石) and find a new base. Despite hardships, the march strengthened the CCP, solidifying Mao's leadership and contributing to the success of the CCP in the civil war. The Long March is considered as a symbol of the resilience of the CCP and is said to have laid the groundwork for the success of the Communist Revolution in China.
4. The students' protest against government rulers for a more democratic regime and its tragic ending still remains a taboo topic in mainland China and the movement is still unmentionable in public discussions, therefore there are very few relevant documentations and papers available in Chinese. For more details about the student protest in 1989 in English, see Zhang *et al.* (2001). For a more general historical context around this movement and its influence, see Lee (2012a).
5. The Asian Games, initiated in 1951, is a multi-sport event held every four years, bringing together athletes from across Asia to compete in a wide range of disciplines. It serves as a platform for cultural exchange and sportsmanship, fostering unity and cooperation among Asian nations.

6. See conversations edited in the book by Cui Jian 崔健 and Zhou Guoping 周国平, 《自由风格》 [*The Free Style*] (2001).

7. See Zha (2006).

8. 'Globalised mass culture' refers to the phenomenon where cultural products, practices, and values are disseminated and consumed on a global scale, often leading to a homogenisation or standardisation of cultural expressions. This process is often driven by advancements in communication, technology, and media, facilitating the widespread circulation of cultural content across national borders. See Featherstone (1990).

9. From the inside pages of the first fanzine in mainland China, *Pop Music Bus*, translated by the author of the book.

10. All the following texts are extracts from different issues of the 'conversation on rock', published in the Chinese magazine titled *Audio&Video World* (音像世界) between June 1992 and October 1994. To enhance readability, the extracts presented here are solely the English translations of the original Chinese texts by the author of the book. The complete column is available as digital resources on the website (https://scream4life.hypotheses.org/704), produced by the author of this book and archived by Nathanel Amar (Accessed 25 May 2024).

11. All the following texts are extracts from Zhao's 赵健伟, 《崔健, 在一无所有中呐喊-中国摇滚备忘录》 (1992). To enhance readability, the extracts presented here are solely the English translations of the original Chinese texts by the author of the book.

12. These extracts of lyrics are translated from Chinese to English by the author from the lyrics of 'A Dream Return to Tang Dynasty' 《梦回唐朝》, featured in the album of Tang Dynasty with the same name *A Dream Return to Tang Dynasty*.

13. See the interview with Gene Lau, 馬高, 麥. '歲月無聲又如歌 – 專訪填詞人劉卓輝'. inmediahk.net. https://www.inmediahk.net/node/1023348, retrieved 25 October 2015 (Accessed 24 July 2024).

14. All the following quotations are extracts from the letter written by Zhang Peiren, attached at the end of the documentary titled *Rock China: The Power of Music* (Qiu 1995). To enhance readability, the extracts presented here are solely the English translations of the original Chinese texts by the author of the book.
15. These extracts of lyrics are translated from Chinese to English by the author from songs featured in the album of 'The Three Prodigies' released by Magic Stone.
16. These extracts of lyrics are translated from Chinese to English by the author from the song titled 'This Is Our Time!' 《这是我们的时代》 by New Pants (新裤子), featured in the album of *Modern Sky I* (摩登天空I), released by Modern Sky Records in 1998.
17. The following quotations are taken from the preface of the book *New Sound of Beijing* (Nie *et al.*, 1999), and the quotations presented here are English translations of the original Chinese texts by the author of the book.
18. China was once the world's largest importer of plastic waste, accounting for nearly 60 per cent of global waste plastics trade. For decades, Western countries, particularly the United States and members of the European Union, exported significant amounts of their plastic waste to China. By the early 2000s, China was receiving nearly 70 per cent of the world's plastic waste, amounting to millions of tons annually (Brooks *et al.*, 2018). Much of this waste included unsold or discarded media, such as CDs and cassettes, which were deemed unsellable in Western markets and were marked with a 'cut-out' notch to prevent official resale. These discarded items were repurposed by Chinese music fans, fueling underground music culture and shaping the so-called *Dakou* generation. However, in 2018, China implemented the 'National Sword' policy, effectively banning the import of most foreign waste, bringing an end to this practice (Liu et al., 2018).

19. Transcripts of stories told by Daodao, translated from Chinese by the author of the book. Lei Peng < babynumb@gmail.com >'About *Dakou*' (关于打口), message sent to < wuyamusic@yahoo.com.cn >, 20–24 March 2010.

20. Both quotes are extracts from a collection of interviews with people who were in some way involved in the *Dakou* phenomenon, translated from Chinese into English by the author. For the integrity of the interviews, see the online article 'Looking for the *Dakou* generation', at https://www.douban.com/group/topic/1002172/?_i=3842690dKHOqDA (Accessed 16 August 2024).

21. The 'Nine-Year Compulsory Education' (九年制义务教育) system in China mandates that all children receive nine years of formal education, typically consisting of six years of primary school and three years of junior secondary school. Introduced in 1986 under the Compulsory Education Law, this policy aims to provide universal access to basic education, improve literacy rates, and promote social and economic development. Education during these nine years is free, though families may need to cover some additional costs, such as for textbooks or uniforms. This system has significantly improved educational access and equity across China.

References

Amar, N. (2018) 'The lives of *Dakou* in China: From waste to Nostalgia', *Études Chinoises*, 38(2), pp. 35–60. DOI: 10.3406/etchi.2018.1647.

Attali, J. (1985) *Noise: The Political Economy of Music*. Translated by B. Massumi. Minneapolis: University of Minnesota Press.

Attali, J. (2001) *Bruits: Essai sur l'économie politique de la musique*. New ed. Paris: Presses Universitaires de France and Librairie Arthème Fayard.

Ball, S. J. (2012) *Global Education Inc.: New Policy Networks and the Neoliberal Imaginary*. New York: Routledge.

Barthes, R. (1957) *Mythologies*. Paris: Seuil.

Barton, D., Chen, Y., and Jin, A. (2024) *Mapping China's Middle class: Generational Change and the Rising Prosperity of Inland Cities Will Power Consumption for Years to Come*. Available at: https://www.mckinsey.com/~/media/McKinsey/Industries/Retail/Our%20Insights/Mapping%20Chinas%20middle%20class/Mapping%20Chinas%20middle%20class.pdf [Accessed 24 October 2024].

Berman, M. (1982) *All That Is Solid Melts into Air: The Experience of Modernity*. New York: Penguin Books.

Berman, M. (1970) *The Politics of Authenticity: Radical Individualism and the Emergence of Modern Society*. New York: Atheneum.

Bhabha, H. K. (1994) *The Location of Culture*. London: Routledge.

Billeter, J. -F. (2000) *Chine trois fois muette: Essai sur l'histoire contemporaine et la Chine, suivi de: Bref essai sur l'histoire de Chine, d'après Spinoza*. Paris: Éditions Allia.

Bislev, A. (2015) 'The Chinese dream: Imagining China', *Fudan Journal of the Humanities and Social Sciences*, 8, pp. 585–595.

Bodhi, Bhikkhu (2000) *The Connected Discourses of the Buddha: A Translation of the Samyutta Nikaya*. Somerville, MA: Wisdom Publications.

Bourdieu, P. (1984) *Distinction: A Social Critique of the Judgement of Taste*. Cambridge, MA: Harvard University Press.

Bourdieu, P. (1986) 'The forms of capital', in Richardson, J. (ed.), *Handbook of Theory and Research for the Sociology of Education*. New York: Greenwood Press, pp. 241–258.

Bourdieu, P. (1996) *The State Nobility: Elite Schools in the Field of Power*. Cambridge: Polity Press.

Bradley, F. (2024) *The Rise of Music Festivals in Asia*. Available at: https://www.burdaluxury.com/insights/the-rise-of-music-festivals-in-asia/ [Accessed 24 August 2024].

Brooks, A. L., Wang, S., and Jambeck, J. R. (2018) 'The Chinese import ban and its impact on global plastic waste trade', *Science Advances*, 4(6), eaat0131.

Brown, W. (2015) *Undoing the Demos: Neoliberalism's Stealth Revolution*. New York: Zone Books.

Campbell, J. (2011) *Red Rock: The Long, Strange March of Chinese Rock and Roll*. Hong Kong: Earnshaw Books.

Capdeville-Zeng, C. (2001) *Rites et rock à Pékin: tradition et modernité de la musique rock dans la société chinoise*. Paris: Les Indes Savantes.

Castells, M. (2010) *The Rise of the Network Society*. 2nd ed. Oxford: Wiley-Blackwell.

Castoriadis, C. (1975) *L'institution imaginaire de la société*. Paris: Seuil.

Castoriadis, C. (1979) *Capitalisme moderne et révolution*. Tome II. Paris: Union Générale d'Édition.

China Internet Network Information Center (CNNIC) (2024) *The 53rd Statistical Report on China's Internet Development*. Available at: http://www.cnnic.cn/ [Accessed 24 August 2024].

Choukroune, L. and Garapon, A. (2007) 'The norms of Chinese harmony: Disciplinary rules as social stabiliser – A harmonious society is one in which the rule of law is given greater strength and authority', *China Perspectives*, 3. Published online 1 September 2010. Available at: http://journals.openedition.org/chinaperspectives/2013 [Accessed 28 October 2019]. DOI: 10.4000/chinaperspectives.2013.

Churchward, D. (2019) *Recent Trends in Modern Foreign Language Exam Entries in Anglophone Countries*. Available at: https://assets.publishing.service.gov.uk/government/uploads/system/uploads/attachment_data/file/844128/Recent_trends_in_modern_foreign_language_exam_entries_in_anglophone_countries_-_FINAL65573.pdf [Accessed 6 November 2024].

Cui, J. 崔健 and Zhou, G. P. 周国平 (2001) 《自由风格》 [*The Free Style*]. 桂林：广西师范大学出版社

Dai, JH. 戴锦华 (2006) 《文化的位置》 ['The position of culture'], 《学术月刊》 [*Academic Monthly*], 38(11), pp. 153–158.

Debord, G. (1967) *La société du spectacle*. Paris: Buchet-Chastel.

Featherstone, M. (1990) *Global Culture: Nationalism, Globalization, and Modernity*. London: Sage Publications.

Foucault, M. (1980) *Power/Knowledge: Selected Interviews and Other Writings, 1972–1977*. Edited by C. Gordon. New York: Pantheon Books.

Freeland, G. (2023) *Music and Black Community in Segregated North Carolina*. New York: Lived Places.

Friedman, T. L. (2005) *The World Is Flat: A Brief History of the Twenty-First Century*. New York: Farrar, Straus and Giroux.

Frith, S. and Horne, H. (1984) 'Welcome to Bohemia!', *Warwick Working Papers in Sociology*. Coventry: University of Warwick.

Glissant, É. (1997) *Poetics of Relation*. Translated by B. Wing. Ann Arbor: University of Michigan Press.

Groenewegen, J. (2005) *Tongue: Making Sense of Underground Rock, Beijing 1997–2004*. MA thesis. Leiden: Leiden University.

Guo, F. C. 郭发财 (2007) 《枷锁与奔跑: 1980–2005 中国摇滚乐独立文化生态观察》 [*Shackled and Running: Observations on the Cultural Ecology of Chinese Rock Indie Culture, 1980–2005*]. 武汉：湖北人民出版社.

Hagström, L. and Nordin, A. H. M. (2020) 'China's "politics of harmony" and the quest for soft power in international politics', *International Studies Review*, 22(3), pp. 507–525. DOI: 10.1093/isr/viz023.

Hall-Lew, L. A. (2002) *English Loanwords in Mandarin Chinese*. PhD thesis. Arizona: University of Arizona.

Hao, F. 郝舫 (1996) 《灿烂涅槃: 柯特柯本的一生》 [*Nirvana Grandiose: The Life of Kurt Cobain*]. 1st ed. 北京：中国社会科学出版社. [2nd ed. 1998; 3rd ed. 2006].

Harari, Y. N. (2015) *Sapiens: A Brief History of Humankind*. New York: HarperCollins.

Harvey, D. (2005) *A Brief History of Neoliberalism*. Oxford: Oxford University Press.Heywood, A. (1994) *Political Ideas and Concepts: An Introduction*. London: Macmillan.

hooks, b. (1984) *Feminist Theory: From Margin to Center*. New York: Routledge.

hooks, b. (1992) *Black Looks: Race and Representation*. New York: Routledge.

Jin, Z. J. 金兆钧 (2002) 《光天化日下的流行: 亲历中国流行音乐》 [*The Rise of Pop under Broad Daylight: A Firsthand Experience of Chinese Popular Music*]. 北京:人民音乐出版社..

Jones, A. F. (1992) *Like a Knife: Ideology and Genre in Contemporary Chinese Popular Music*. New York: East Asia Program, Cornell University.

Jones, M. L. (2008) 'Review article: The country blues – music and identities in different Americas', *Journal of Contemporary History*, 43(4), pp. 711–721. DOI: 10.1177/0022009408095426.

Jung, C. G. (1959) *The Archetypes and the Collective Unconscious*. Translated by R. F. C. Hull. Princeton, NJ: Princeton University Press. (Collected Works, Vol. 9, Part 1).

Jung, C. G. (1968) *The Structure and Dynamics of the Psyche*. Translated by R. F. C. Hull. Princeton, NJ: Princeton University Press. (Collected Works, Vol. 8).

Kaminski, J. S. (2024) 'Symbolic Changes in Modern Chinese Military Bands from Westernization to Revolution (c. 1895 to c. 1937)', *International Review of the Aesthetics and Sociology of Music*, 55(2), pp. 283–304. Available at: https://www.jstor.org/stable/48801074 [Accessed 7 August 2024].

Kierkegaard, S. (1847) *The Journals of Søren Kierkegaard*, ed. and trans. by Dru, A. (1959), London: Oxford University Press. Entry no. 618, X1 A 354.

Laozi (1997) *Tao Te Ching: A Book About the Way and the Power of the Way*. Translated by Ursula K. Le Guin. Boston: Shambhala.

Lee, G. B. (2002) *La Chine et le Spectre de l'Occident: Contestation Poétique, Modernité et Métissage*. Translated from English by E.U. Saint-André. Paris: Syllepse.

Lee, G. B. (2012a) *China's Lost Decade: Cultural Politics and Poetics 1978–1990 in Place of History*. Brookline, MA: Zephyr Press; Lyon: Éditions Tigre de Papier.

Lee, G. B. (2012b) 'Le cadeau empoisonné de Versailles ou la Chine à la manivelle de l'orgue de barbarie', *Mouvements*, 72, pp. 79–88.

Lee, G .B. (2012c) *Un spectre hante la Chine: Fondements de la contestation actuelle. Une histoire politico-culturelle 1978–1990*. Lyon: Tigre de Papier. DOI: 10.3917/mouv.072.0079.

Liu, J. (2024) 'Internet censorship in China: Looking through the lens of categorisation', *Journal of Current Chinese Affairs*, 0(0). DOI: https://doi.org/10.1177/18681026231220948.

Liu, K., Adams, M., Walker, T. R., and Rintoul, L. (2018) 'The National Sword policy: China's response to global plastic waste trade', *Environmental Science & Policy*, 93, pp. 8–11.

Lu, M. H. 卢美慧 (2021) 《沈黎晖 茫茫荒野漫游》[*Shen Lihui: Wanderings in the Munchkin Wilderness*) 博雅天下 (*Boya Tianxia* Media Group), 18 January. Available at: https://www.boyamedia.com/category/detail/14405/ [Accessed 7 August 2024].

Nāgārjuna (1995) *The Fundamental Wisdom of the Middle Way: Nāgārjuna's Mūlamadhyamakakārikā*. Translated by J. L. Garfield. New York: Oxford University Press.

Nie, Z. 聂筝, Yan, J. 颜峻 and Ou, N. 欧宁 (eds) (1999) 《北京新声》（*New Sound of Beijing*).长沙：湖南文艺出版社.

Noebel, D. A. (1966) *Rhythm, Riots, and Revolution: An Analysis of the Communist Use of Music, the Communist Master Music Plan*. Tulsa, OK: Christian Crusade Publications.

Ong, A. (2006) *Neoliberalism as Exception: Mutations in Citizenship and Sovereignty*. Durham, NC: Duke University Press.

Rutkevich, N. (2023) 'The growth of social tension and the change of protest movements in France', *Valdai Discussion Club*. Available at: https://valdaiclub.com/a/highlights/the-growth-of-social-tension-in-france/ [Accessed 26 February 2025].

Said, E. W. (1978) *Orientalism*. New York: Pantheon Books.

Said, E. W. (1993) *Culture and Imperialism*. New York: Vintage Books.

Sen, G. and Grown, C. (1987) *Development, Crises, and Alternative Visions: Third World Women's Perspectives*. New York: Monthly Review Press.

Srnicek, N. (2017) *Platform Capitalism*. Cambridge: Polity Press.

Steen, A. (2000) 'Sound, protest and business: Modern Sky Co. and the new ideology of Chinese rock', *Berliner China-Hefte*, 18, pp. 40–64.

Steen, A. (2011) 'Long Live the Revolution? The Changing Spirit of Chinese Rock', in Peddie, I. (ed.) *Popular Music and Human Rights, Volume II: World Music,* pp. 131–146.

Taishō Tripitaka, T251, *Prajñāpāramitāhṛdaya Sūtra* 《般若波罗蜜多心经》. Translated by Xuanzang 玄奘, 7th century CE.

Taylor, C. (1985) 'Atomism', in Taylor, C. (ed.) *Philosophical Papers. Volume 2: Philosophy and the Human Sciences*. Cambridge: Cambridge University Press, pp. 187–210.

Thich Nhat Hanh (2017) *The Other Shore: A New Translation of the Heart Sutra with Commentaries*. Berkeley: Palm Leaves Press.

Uhm, Y. (2021) 'Plastic waste trade in Southeast Asia after China's import ban: Implications of the new Basel Convention amendment and recommendations for the future', *California Western Law Review*, 57(1), Article 2. Available at: https://scholarlycommons.law.cwsl.edu/cwlr/vol57/iss1/2 [Accessed 16 August 2024].

Wang, M. Z. 王莫之 (2020a) '《音像世界》：红布，传教士，诸神的黄昏（一）' ['Audio & Video World: Red rags, evangelists, and the twilight of the gods' – I], *The Paper* 澎湃新闻, 23 January. Available at: https://m.thepaper.cn/kuaibao_detail.jsp?contid=5574292 [Accessed 1 August 2024].

Wang, M. Z. 王莫之 (2020b) '《音像世界》：红布，传教士，诸神的黄昏（二）' ['Audio & Video World: Red rags, evangelists, and the twilight of the gods' – II], *The Paper* 澎湃新闻, 31 January.

Available at: https://m.thepaper.cn/kuaibao_detail.jsp?contid=5611289 [Accessed 1 August 2024].

Wang, M. Z. 王莫之 (2020c) '《音像世界》：红布，传教士，诸神的黄昏（三）' ['Audio & Video World: Red rags, evangelists, and the twilight of the gods' – III], *The Paper* 澎湃新闻, 8 February. Available at: https://m.thepaper.cn/newsDetail_forward_5758753 [Accessed 1 August 2024].

Weller, S. (1969) 'Jimi Hendrix: I don't want to be a clown anymore', *Rolling Stone*, 15 November. Available at: https://www.rocksbackpages.com/Library/Article/jimi-hendrix-i-dont-want-to-be-a-clown-any-more- [Accessed 16 April 2025].

Weller, S. and Frith, S. (1984) 'Welcome to Bohemia!', *Warwick Working Papers in Sociology*. Coventry: University of Warwick.

Wicke, P. (1990) *Rock Music: Culture, Aesthetics and Sociology*. Translated by R. Fogg. Cambridge: Cambridge University Press.

Williams, A. K., Owens, L., and Syedullah, J. C. (2016) *Radical Dharma: Talking Race, Love, and Liberation*. Berkeley: North Atlantic Books.

Xu, G. (2011) *Strangers on the Western Front: Chinese Workers in the Great War*. Cambridge, MA: Harvard University Press.

Yan, J. 颜峻 (2002) 《地地下：新音乐潜行记》 [*Underground: A Quiet Journey into the World of New Music*]. 北京：文化艺术出版社.

Zha, J. Y. 查建英 (2006) 《八十年代访谈录》 [*The Eighties*]. 北京：三联书店.

Zhang, L. (comp.), Nathan, A. J. and Link, P. (eds), with an afterword by Schell, O. (2001) *The Tiananmen Papers: The Chinese Leadership's Decision to Use Force Against Their Own People – In Their Own Words*. New York: PublicAffairs.

Zhao, J. W. 赵健伟 (1992) 《崔健, 在一无所有中呐喊: 中国摇滚备忘录》 [*Cui Jian, Screaming in the Midst of Nothing – Chinese Rock Memo*]. Beijing: Beijing Normal University Press.

Zuboff, S. (2019) *The Age of Surveillance Capitalism*. New York: Public Affairs.

《打口故乡寻根记》 ['Finding the roots of Dakou in its hometown'] (2001) *So Rock!* 《我爱摇滚乐》, 11, pp. 12–15.

《寻找打口一代》 ['Looking for the Dakou generation'] (n.d.) Douban.com. Available at: https://www.douban.com/group/topic/1002172/ [Accessed 16 August 2024].

Multimedia References

Nalin, P. (2001) Samsara [Film]. Paris: Pandora Film/Monsoon Films/Pathé International.

Qiu, L. T. 邱礼涛 (1995) *Rock China: The Power of Music* 《摇滚中国乐势力》 [VCD]. Hong Kong: Magic Stone Records.

Radiolab (2021) *Dakou: Mixtape*. 22 October. [Podcast]. Available at: https://radiolab.org/podcast/mixtape-dakou [Accessed 19 August 2024].

Recommended further readings

Baldwin, J. (1963) *The Fire Next Time*. New York: Dial Press.

Dai, J. H. 戴锦华 (1999) 《隐形书写：90年代中国文化研究》 [*Invisible Writing: Cultural Studies in 1990s China*]. 南京: 江苏人民出版社.

Dai, J. H. 戴锦华 (2007) 《性别中国》 [*Gendering China*]. 台北: 麦田出版.

Dai, J. H. 戴锦华 (2002) *Cinema and Desire: Feminist Marxism and Cultural Politics in the Work of Dai Jinhua*. Edited by J. Wang and T. E. Barlow. London: Verso.

Dai, J. H. 戴锦华 (2018) *After the Post-Cold War: The Future of Chinese History*. Durham, NC: Duke University Press.

Fanon, F. (1952) *Black Skin, White Masks*. Translated by C. L. Markmann. New York: Grove Press.

Fanon, F. (1961) *The Wretched of the Earth*. Translated by R. Philcox. New York: Grove Press.

Foucault, M. (1966) *The Order of Things: An Archaeology of the Human Sciences*. New York: Pantheon Books.

Foucault, M. (1977) *Discipline and Punish: The Birth of the Prison*. Translated by A. Sheridan. New York: Vintage Books.

hooks, b. (1984) *Feminist Theory: From Margin to Center*. Boston, MA: South End Press.

hooks, b. (1994) *Outlaw Culture: Resisting Representations*. New York: Routledge.

hooks, b. (2000) *All About Love: New Visions*. New York: William Morrow.

hooks, b. (2004) *The Will to Change: Men, Masculinity, and Love*. New York: Simon&Schuster.

Roy, A. (2001) *Power Politics*. Cambridge, MA: South End Press.

Roy, A. (2014) *Capitalism: A Ghost Story*. Chicago: Haymarket Books.

Ueno, C. (2004) *Nationalism and Gender*. Translated by B. Yamamoto. Melbourne: Trans Pacific Press.

Ueno, C. (2016) *The Politics of Memory: Nation, Individual and Self*. Translated by N. Sakai. New York: Routledge.

Ueno, C. (2020) *On Women*. Translated by B. Yamamoto. New York: Verso.

Varoufakis, Y. (2023) *Technofeudalism: What Killed Capitalism*. London: Bodley Head.

Recommended films or documentaries about Chinese rock

Guan, H. 管虎 (1994) 《头发乱了》 [*Dirt*]. China.

Lindt, G. and Messmer, S. (2005) 《北京浪花》 [*Beijing Bubbles*]. Germany.

Lu, X. C. 路学长 (1997) 《长大成人》 [*The Making of Steel*]. China.

Manceaux, F. and Schwerfel, H. P. (1993) *Rock in Berlin 1993: The Chinese Avant-Garde* (中国摇滚在柏林), Continental Cameras, China.

Sheng, Z. M. 盛志民 (2009) 《再见乌托邦》 [*Night of an Era*]. China.

Wu, W. G. 吴文光 (2001) 《流浪北京》 [*Wandering Beijing*]. China.

Zhang, Y. 张扬 (2001) 《昨天》 [*Quitting*]. China.

Zhang, Y. 张扬 (2005) 《后革命时代》 [*Post-Revolutionary Era*]. China.

A comprehensive discography of Chinese rock, folk, and alternative music is included as an appendix in Lei Peng's doctoral thesis, *Rock in China: Contestation and Consumption Since the 1980s* (written in French). The thesis is openly accessible via the French academic repository **Sudoc**.

Permanent link (Sudoc): https://www.sudoc.fr/189173750

Index

A Dream Return to Tang Dynasty 71, 224

anattā (non-self) xiv, 210

Audio&Video World 52–54, 56–58, 224

bell hooks xiii, 193

capitalist modernity 198, 201

'centre' xi, 19, 29, 62, 125, 126, 151, 164, 213

'China Fire' 69–94

Chinese rock ix, xi, xiv, xix, xx, xxi, xxiv, 2, 4, 6, 7, 9–12, 15, 16, 18, 20, 25, 26, 28, 29, 32, 39, 41, 42, 45, 47, 51–53, 57, 63, 64, 73, 75, 78, 79, 83, 84, 92, 97, 98, 105–108, 116, 122–125, 139, 140, 150, 164–166, 178, 193, 195, 197, 201, 204, 205, 209, 211, 212, 220–222

collective ego 212

'conversation on rock' 57–64, 224

'cross-cultural identity' xix, 127, 197, 209, 211, 214, 215, 220

Cultural Revolution xxii, 5, 9, 23, 37, 46–48, 114, 198, 207

Dai Jinhua xiii, xv, 17

Dakou 50, 52, 95, 98–100, 102, 103, 105–118, 121, 122, 133, 137

'Dakou generation' 106, 107, 110, 113–118

'Dakou youth' 116

Deng Xiaoping 5, 10, 49, 198

Du Fu 72

Earth Records 74, 75, 77, 83

Édouard Glissant 211

Edward Said xiii, 162

Enlightenment ix, 17, 18, 37, 64, 86, 133, 154, 155, 160–162, 166, 207

'Establish yourself at the age of thirty' 174

Eurocentrism 154, 160, 161

fluid belonging 213

Folksongs on Campus 74, 75

Four Modernisations 199

freedom of invisibility 210

Gene Lau 74, 75, 224

Gregory Lee xv, 10, 161, 178, 198

Guy Debord 121, 123

Hao Fang 106–109

'harmonious society' 115, 116

Heart Sutra 182, 233
He Yong 76, 78, 87, 88
HLM 155, 157–160, 164, 208, 214
hybrid system of domination 194
ideology xiv, xvi, xxiv, 6, 7, 12, 20, 24, 28, 46, 47, 49, 59, 62, 64, 66, 93, 115, 116, 202
imperialist supremacist feudal patriarchy 194
imperialist white supremacist capitalist patriarchy 194
integration xiii, xix, xxiv, 13, 25, 52, 73, 119, 125, 197, 208, 209, 212
interdependence xiii, xiv, 166, 182, 211, 215
interlocking system of power 191
'invisible Chinese rock' 201
'Iron Rice Bowl' 90

Kurt Cobain 106–108

'leftover woman' 176
Leslie Chan Kin Tim 73
'liberal world' 169, 173, 180, 181, 192

Magic Stone 71, 73–78, 81, 83, 87, 88, 94
Mao Zedong 5, 25, 148
Midi Music Academy 140
Modern Sky 25, 67, 69–94, 96, 123, 225

'model opera' 46
myth ix, xxiii, 18, 25, 27–33, 35–39, 41, 42, 46, 47, 49, 52, 57–60, 62–67, 70, 74, 76, 80, 83, 84, 92, 94, 97, 106–109, 122, 124, 135, 142, 146, 150, 154, 158, 164, 165, 171, 179, 182, 183, 198, 202, 205, 207, 211, 214
myth of rock 27–30, 57, 63, 64, 70, 107, 146, 154, 164, 171, 205, 207
myth of yaogun 41–67, 124

'neoliberalisation of education' 184
neoliberalism x, 173, 183, 190, 193, 198, 213
'New Sound of Beijing' 95–119
'Nothing to My Name' 20, 21, 32, 217, 223
Nirvana 57, 106, 108, 112, 230
No. 43 Baojiajie Road 4, 5, 97

Opium War 42, 199
Orientalism 162
'Other' ix, xii, xix, xxiii, 50, 160, 162, 188, 208, 211, 213
Ou Ning 96, 97, 99
'only child' 129, 200

'periphery' xi, 41, 48, 62, 152, 209
Pierre Bourdieu 189
'post-70s' 77
'post-80s' 77, 170

practice of not belonging 215

pratītyasamutpāda (dependent origination) 214

Red Star Records 73–75, 77

reform and opening up 5–7, 9, 45, 49, 58, 83

Relation 126, 208, 211

revolutionary ix, xxii, 3, 5, 10, 24, 27–30, 32, 33, 35, 37–39, 43–45, 47, 49, 52, 59, 62–67, 70, 92, 94, 122, 144, 153, 154, 202, 205

'Rock China: the Power of Music' 78

Rock 'N' Roll on the New Long March 19, 21, 22, 70

Romantic individualism 37, 58

Shen Lihui 25, 92–94, 96, 97, 232

silence of China 201

Sober 25, 89, 91, 92, 96, 97

social capital xi, 153, 187, 189, 190, 213

social hierarchies 156, 157, 185, 189, 193, 198

spectacle 121, 123, 229

'spectre of the West' 198

śūnyatā (emptiness) xiv, 210

symbolic capital 189, 190

Tang Dynasty 70–73, 75, 76, 78, 89, 94, 224

The Long March 25, 223

'The Three Prodigies' 75, 76, 78, 87, 89

the Midi Music Festival 124, 138, 141, 146

Wang Xiaofeng 56, 57, 62, 66

Wudaokou 132, 133, 137

Yan Jun 96, 116

Yaogun xvi, 4, 6, 9, 12, 15, 18, 28, 39, 41, 45, 46, 47, 49, 59, 62, 64–67, 70, 71, 73–80, 82–85, 87, 89, 91–94, 96, 97, 101, 122–124, 129, 131, 136, 138–140, 142, 146, 154, 164, 195, 197–199, 201–207, 209

Zhang Chu 4, 76, 78, 88

Zhang Fan 139, 143

Zhang Lei 57, 66

Zhang Peiren 71, 73, 74, 78–80, 82, 88, 225

Zhao Jianwei 64

Zhongguancun 132

www.ingramcontent.com/pod-product-compliance
Lightning Source LLC
Chambersburg PA
CBHW070758230426
43665CB00017B/2403